PRAGUE WALKS

Frank Kuznik

DUNCAN PETERSEN

gpp®
travel

Guilford, Connecticut

W0010192

Copyright © 2010 Duncan Petersen Publishing Ltd

Conceived, designed and produced by
Duncan Petersen Publishing Limited
C7, Old Imperial Laundry
Warriner Gardens, London SW11 4XW
United Kingdom

Published in the USA by
Globe Pequot Press
Guilford, Connecticut

UK ISBN-13: 978-1-903301-53-1
US ISBN-13: 978-0-7627-4844-0

A CIP catalogue record for this book is available from the British Library.
Library of Congress Cataloging-in-Publication Data is available.

The right of Frank Kuznik to be identified as the author of this work has been asserted by him in
accordance with the Copyright, Designs and Patents Act 1988.

Conceived, designed and produced by
Duncan Petersen Publishing Ltd

Editorial Director Andrew Duncan

Editor Rachel Piercey

Maps Advanced Illustrations Ltd., Thomas Coulson

Photographs Frank Kuznik, Futaba Tanaka

Printed by Butler Tanner & Dennis, UK

**Visit Duncan Petersen's travel website at
www.charmingsmallhotels.co.uk**

4

CONTENTS

Exploring Prague on foot

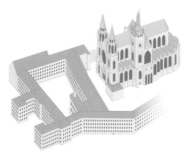

With centuries-old art, architecture and living history on almost every block, Prague is a city made for walking. Though the city proper encompasses about 500 square kilometers (193 square miles), its historic centre is relatively compact, easily traversed in two or three relaxed days. Public transport in Prague is efficient and easily accessible (once you've mastered the perplexing ticket system), and almost all the walks in this book begin and end at convenient tram or metro stops. But to truly experience the city and discover its many hidden treasures, you should explore it on foot.

Getting lost is a common experience in Prague, particularly in the labyrinthine medieval streets of Old Town. Don't let this deter you from being adventurous. You have not properly experienced Prague if you haven't stopped at some point, wondered where you are, pulled out a map and started searching for the elusive street signs. Everyone who visits the city has these moments, and they often lead to unexpected surprises – a quiet lane, a charming café or a breathtaking sculpture not marked on any map. And in a city of Prague's size, you can't stay lost for long.

The historic part of Prague is divided roughly into two main areas: Malá Strana, the 'lesser quarter', on the west side of the river, and Staré Město (Old Town) on the east side. Prague Castle is the historic heart of Malá Strana, which also includes the neighbourhoods behind and below the castle, and Petřín hill. On the other side of the Vltava River, Josefov (the Jewish Quarter) is part of Old Town, which is flanked to the east

HOW THE MAPPING WAS MADE

A small team of specialist cartographers created the maps digitally in Adobe Illustrator. The footprint of the buildings is drawn first, then the width of the streets is artificially increased in order to give extra space for the buildings to be drawn in three dimensions. Next, the buildings are added, using aerial photography as reference. Finally the details of the buildings and the colour is added - the first very time consuming, the second less so because digital drawing programmes allow it to be automated.

and south by New Town (Nové Město). The walks in this book also take you further afield, to points of interest along the river and to less-developed areas east of Old Town, which are rapidly disappearing as the Czech Republic shakes off the last vestiges of communism and becomes increasingly Westernized.

The unique aerial-view (isometric) mapping used in this guide makes it easier to use than flat maps, because you can locate yourself by the look of the buildings, as well as the street plan. The unique look of the maps brings *ulice* (streets), *náměstí* (squares), individual buildings and even neighbourhoods to life. Routes are clearly marked on the maps and brief directions help you to follow the route. The numerals on the maps are waymarks, linked to route directions and to information about places of interest in the text.

The walks are designed to show you the many facets of the city, from the grandest achievements of Bohemian culture to the dispiriting remnants of totalitarianism, with glittery new shops, hotels and other showcases of capitalism marking the march of global commerce. The latter seem to spring up overnight, so don't be surprised by jarring juxtapositions not mentioned in this book. Even the locals have a hard time keeping up with the latest fast-food franchise or urban gear store that's set up shop in an historic landmark building.

Most of the walks can be done in an hour, though they are packed with plenty to see and a wealth of places where you can stop and refresh yourself. So if the weather is fine and you are inclined to linger at the Castle gardens or settle in for some serious people-watching in Old Town Square, by all means do. A city with a history as proud and deep as Prague's deserves to be savoured. Take all 12 walks at an unhurried pace, and you will come away with a new understanding and appreciation of Central European history and culture, and an intimate view of a society still very much in transition.

HOW TO USE THIS BOOK

The area covered by the walks encompasses the entire historic centre of Prague, from Old Town's northern border along the Vltava to the Botanical Gardens on the south end of New Town, and from Florence on the east end of New Town to Hradčany, the western edge of Malá Strana. The Riverfront Walk and Vyšehrad Circuit take you out of the city centre to some less-travelled, but attractive and historically significant points south.

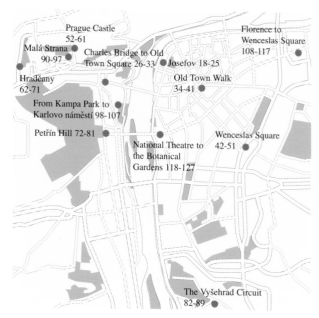

Prague Castle 52-61
Malá Strana 90-97
Charles Bridge to Old Town Square 26-33
Josefov 18-25
Florence to Wenceslas Square 108-117
Hradčany 62-71
Old Town Walk 34-41
From Kampa Park to Karlovo náměstí 98-107
Petřín Hill 72-81
National Theatre to the Botanical Gardens 118-127
Wenceslas Square 42-51
The Vyšehrad Circuit 82-89

Using the maps

The route of each walk is clearly marked on the map, with arrows to point you in the right direction. The guide also tells you where the walk starts and ends, indicating the nearest metro or subway stop, which is never more than a few minutes' walk away. Numerals on the maps correspond to the numerals in the text, marking the start of each section of the walk. They will help you to keep your bearings. **Bold print** alerts you to points of interest on the route that follow in the order mentioned. Bold is also used to indicate other interesting places nearby, such as museums, galleries, statues, restaurants, bars or shops. For more information on admission to sights, see page 15.

LINKING THE WALKS

Almost all the walks are within easy reach of each other (if not by foot, then metro or tram), with the exception of **Green Retreat** and **Myths and Legends**, which are dedicated walks in park areas outside of the city centre where you can enjoy the greenery and spectacular views. The first four walks – **Power and the Glory, Luxurious palaces, Origins of a City** and **Old Town Walk** – form a continuous link that takes you through the regal neighborhoods of the 'lesser quarter', across Charles Bridge and through Old Town. Along the way you will pass **Prague Castle**, which deserves time of its own, and links up nicely with **The Jewish Quarter**, by walking across the Mánes bridge. **Communist Relics**, which starts at the furthest point east, fits naturally with **Historic Heart**. And the **Riverfront Walk**, which starts below the west end of the Charles Bridge, ends a short tram ride from the National Theatre, the starting point of **New Town**.

THE WEATHER

Prague sits in a geographical bowl at the centre of the Czech Republic, which tends to make the winters milder but the summers hotter. The city has four distinct seasons, with January typically the coldest month. The infrequent snow is lovely, but usually melts quickly, and with the temperature typically hovering around freezing, it can easily turn to rain that coats the sidewalks and streets with ice. Expect rain in the spring, which turns the city a lush green almost overnight, and fills the air with the fragrance of blossom during April. Summers are variable, with stretches of intense heat broken up by thunderstorms that bring cooler temperatures. Autumn comes early and is beautiful, especially on Petřin, where the hillside brims with edible fruits and nuts. October sometimes brings a last week or two of warm weather, but by November the grey skies and cold have settled in for the winter.

WHEN TO USE THIS BOOK

All of these walks can be enjoyed at any time of year, though the city's gardens and parks are at their best in the summer. (Many of the private gardens are closed during the winter months.) Those with many indoor attractions – museums, churches, synagogues – are best saved for cold or rainy days.

Summer walks

• **Prague Castle**: a must-see any time of the year, but in its full glory during the warmer months, when the extensive gardens are lush with greenery and fragrant blossoms. Most visitors tend to stay within the Castle walls, making the gardens a cool, serene retreat, especially in the evenings, when they are often nearly deserted.

• **Luxurious palaces, charming lanes, red roofs**: the view from Prague Castle may be hazy, but summer is when Nerudova Street really hums, with its unique mix of colourful tourist shops, lively pubs, and restaurants with their doors flung open and menus posted on the side of the street. The main attraction of the lower part of the walk, Wallenstein Gardens, is open only during the summer.

• **Historic Heart**: another must-see any time of year, but summer is when you can experience the full breadth and scope of Wenceslas Square, from a majestic St Wenceslas astride his horse to the tourists, touts and sausage stands that are its modern-day lifeblood. Plenty of sidewalk cafés and benches interspersed among the flower beds offer great spots for people-watching.

• **Riverfront Walk**: this will take you through lovely Kampa Park and two islands, Střelecký and Slovansky, which are hubs for boating, fishing and, on some weekends, outdoor music festivals during the summer. As the gaggle of tour boats suggests, some of the best views of Prague are from the river.

• **Myths and Legends**: a leafy retreat from the city heat, just two metro stops south of city centre but much cooler and calmer. It has many great observation points of the city, the river and the Castle. Bake in the sun on the ramparts or enjoy a cool drink in one of the tree-shaded cafés.

• **Green Retreat**: crisscrossed by meandering paths and dotted with viewpointss, Petřín hillside is perfect for a short stroll or half a day exploring and admiring the views. For the best view of all, make your way to the top and climb the winding staircase of Petřín Tower.

Winter walks

• **Power and the Glory**: beautiful any time of year, but the stately hush of this regal neighbourhood seems even more pronounced during the winter. Indoor diversions such as

Strahov Monastery and the Loreto will keep you warm and intrigued for as long as you care to stay.

• **Origins of a City** and **Old Town Walk**: the tourist hordes have gone, there's plenty of room in the restaurants and gift shops, and the performing arts calendar is brimming with delights. Especially enchanting during December, when the smell of hot mulled wine wafts over Christmas markets set up at náměstí Republiky, Můstek and Old Town Square.

• **The Jewish Quarter**: the most interesting sights in the Jewish Quarter are inside the synagogues and museums, which offer moving experiences no matter what your nationality, particularly the Old Jewish Cemetery and the Holocaust memorial in the Pinkas synagogue. During American President Barack Obama's visit to Prague in April 2009, this is where his wife Michelle spent her free time.

WEEKEND WALKS

• **Communist Relics** and **New Town**: the workaday crowds have left and the pace on the streets, as well as in shops and restaurants, is much more relaxed. You'll have the time and space to linger, especially to observe architectural details. As for shopping, the newer shops and malls will be open, but for the small curiosity shops, you may have to come back during the week.

• **Riverfront Walk**: the river comes alive on weekends during the summer, so you can join in the fun with, say, a rental boat, or find a shady spot on the banks of the islands to watch it all happen. During the winter, Museum Kampa and the Cathedral of Sts Cyril and Methodius will provide hours of absorbing indoor viewing.

• **Green Retreat**: the many pathways and viewpoints of Petřín hillside make it an ideal place to wander when you have no particular agenda or time constraints. If you're there in the evening, it's also the perfect place to watch the city lights come up at twilight.

• **Myths and Legends**: it's a mystery why more locals don't flock here on weekends, but even on a Sunday afternoon the park offers plenty of open green space and available seating in the cafés. If ever a place was made for a leisurely weekend stroll, this is it.

WEEKDAY WALKS

• **Origins of a City** and **Old Town Walk**: start early to avoid the crush on Charles Bridge and then enjoy the maze of medieval streets, where it's much easier to keep your bearings by daylight during the week. Everything is open, from the tiniest gift shops to the grand museums ringing Old Town Square (except for Monday, when almost all the museums in Prague are closed). The sounds and smells are different on every block.

• **Historic Heart**: the city's commercial hub is best experienced during the week, when it hums with a busy mix of office workers, tourists, shoppers and hustlers. There's always an entertaining show on the street, and a full menu of diversions ranging from the stately National Museum to the glitzy casinos.

WALKS FOR KIDS

• **Prague Castle**: the awe and grandeur of the Castle complex is impressive no matter what your age, and St Vitus Cathedral will almost certainly be the biggest, most impressive building young children have ever seen. You won't have thoughtful time to linger in the galleries with kids in tow, but the Castle courtyards and gardens are a playground for young and old alike.

• **Origins of a City** and **Old Town Walk**: a great idea as long as you've got money to spend on toys and souvenirs, which beckon from the windows of Old Town shops. You're also never more than a few steps from an ice cream stand or café, so you can proceed at a child's pace, with plenty of places at which to pause and refresh along the way.

• **Riverfront Walk**: great parks and open spaces for running wild and free, ducks, gulls and other wildlife along the river, and a delightful playground on the southern end of Slovansky Ostrov make this walk a perfect outing with the kids. If they're adventurous, you can rent a pedal boat and take it to the river.

• **Green Retreat**: another great place to turn the kids loose, with occasional walls and fortified lookout points that are every young boy's dream. If you make it to the top, don't miss the Mirror Maze, a clever funhouse for kids of all ages. Youngsters six and older will also enjoy climbing Petřín Tower.

• **Myths and Legends**: the monuments and churches might not mean much to the younger set, but the battlements and lookout points are straight out of a fairy tale. Look for the playgrounds as well, which are not always obvious but very thoughtfully designed for young children.

GETTING TO PRAGUE

Most of the major European airlines offer service to Prague. Home-based Czech Airlines (ČSA) offers the most direct connections to other European cities, and to selected overseas destinations. At the time of going to press, the budget airlines Easy Jet, Ryanair, Smart Wings and SkyEurope also fly to Prague.

GETTING AROUND

Prague has an extensive subway (called the metro), tram and bus system that is mostly efficient and reliable. However, be forewarned that tram service can change abruptly, with street or rail repairs rerouting or cancelling entire lines for brief periods of time. There is no way to know about these in advance: even locals can be found standing at tram stops with puzzled looks on their faces, trying to decipher a sign with directions

for alternative transport (usually an 'X' bus that travels the same route). Rerouting doesn't occur very often, though, and shouldn't pose major problems.

Mastering the ticketing can be difficult. You must buy a ticket with the appropriate fare in advance, and stamp it with the time by inserting it in one of the small yellow boxes at the escalator entrance of metro stations (on trams and buses, the boxes are mounted inside the vehicles). Often, the hardest part of this is simply finding ticket vending machines, which are prominently posted at all metro entrances but rarely at tram and bus stops. Ticket costs vary according to the amount of time you plan to ride; the basic fee is 18 Czech crowns (Kč) for 20 minutes. For more, check the instructions on the machine, which are printed in English. You would do well to stock up on tickets when you're at a metro station, or consider purchasing a multi-day pass, which you can buy at the I.P. Pavlova and Muzeum metro stations. If they're in stock, it's also worth buying a transport map, which will show you how to get

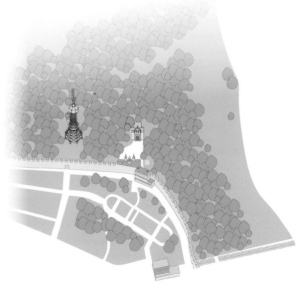

anywhere in the city using public transport.

The temptation to ride without a valid ticket, known locally as 'riding black', is strong. Ticket inspectors patrol the metro cars, trams and buses, but there are not many of them, and you can go days without seeing one. But inevitably, when you least expect it, a plainclothes cop will come up, flash his badge and demand to see your ticket. If you do not have one, you will be fined up to 800 Kč, and there are no excuses. The transport police have heard them all, and they love to prey on ignorant tourists, particularly on the popular 9 and 22 tram lines. If you don't have the money, they will escort you off the tram to the nearest ATM to get it. Spend the 20 or 30 Kč and save yourself a very unpleasant experience.

Another word of caution: organized gangs of pickpockets work the busiest metro and tram lines, particularly in the summer, and will be off with your wallet, purse or camera before you even know it's gone. Be conscious of your bags when riding public transport, don't let them hang open, and don't let yourself be distracted by some commotion in the car – a favourite trick to divert your attention while you are being relieved of your valuables. The city police (*mětská policie*) have heard all those stories, and will have no interest in yours, nor any ambition to apprehend the thieves.

Getting public transport
Another quirk of the Prague transport system is that there is no direct metro connection to the city from the airport. Instead, you need to take the 119 bus to Dejvická, the terminus of the A (green) subway line, which will then take you to city centre. The 119 makes two stops at Ruzyně Airport, in front of terminals 1 and 2

(both stops have ticket machines).

Taxis
If you're carrying a lot of luggage, it will be more expensive but much easier to take a taxi into the city, or one of the Cedaz vans. Either way, the ride will cost you around 500 Kč. You will see the taxis and vans lined up when you step outside the terminals.

Once you're in the city, do not hail a passing taxi or use one parked at a street corner. Prague cabbies are notorious for overcharging tourists, and will take you for a ride in every sense of the term. Instead, call AAA Taxi (222 333 222) or City Taxi (233 103 310), both of which have English-language operators. They will send an honest driver to pick you up. There are also a number of taxi stands in city centre marked 'Fair Place', at which only honest drivers supposedly wait. There have been mixed results of this laudable idea. Try it at your own risk.

TOURIST INFORMATION
Prague Information Services (PIS) dispenses maps, brochures and information on events, accommodation and tours at several locations (the first number refers to the street address and the second to the district within Prague):
• Old Town Hall on Old Town Square, Staroměstské náměstí 1, Prague 1, tel 236 002 562
• Prague Airport, tel 224 247 243
• The main railway station, Hlavní nádrazi, Wilsonova 8, Prague 2
• Charles Bridge tower, Malá Strana side, only in summer
• Rytírská 31, Prague 1

(for the three above call PIS general information, tel 221 714 444) PIS also runs a useful website in six languages at www.prague-info.cz.

Disabled travellers

Once you get out of the airport, there is very little accommodation for wheelchairs in Prague. Cut curbs make some of the street corners easier, and a few of the metro stations have lifts. But most of the pubs and restaurants are accessible only via stairs, and the public toilets are hit-and-miss. The PIS desk at Old Town Hall has an accessibility map that many wheelchair users have found useful. PIS staff will also have information on which tourist sites are most accessible to wheelchair users.

Theatre tickets

Prague's rich cultural life is one of the main reasons to visit the city. Music, opera and dance are your best bets, as almost all local theatre is performed in Czech – even Shakespeare at the Castle during the summer.

The cultural season runs in cycles. There's a lull during January and February, when there's not much happening outside the National Theatre, State Opera and major orchestra halls (Rudolfinum, Obecní dům). The festival season starts to pick up in the spring, with a wealth of music and dance performances capped by the Prague Spring Classical Music Festival in May and early June. The performing arts season starts to taper off in June, and aside from a couple of notable festivals (Prague Proms, Summer

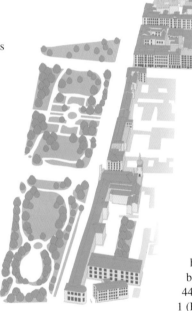

Festivities of Early Music, Dvořák's Prague), there's not much worth seeing during July and August. All the orchestras and opera houses start their regular seasons again in September, and every month during the autumn is strong. The year rounds off with a dazzling month of seasonal music in December.

Tracking down all these events can be a dizzying task if you don't speak Czech. Prague's English-language weekly, *The Prague Post*, offers the city's most comprehensive entertainment listings for visitors (published every Wednesday). You will also find helpful programmes at the various ticket offices. Ticketpro and Ticketstream are the main agencies for rock, pop and jazz concerts, and some sporting events. Sazka Ticket handles most of the arena rock shows. The National Theatre, State Opera and orchestra concert halls all run their own box offices. Selected locations include:

• National Theatre box offices: Ostrovní 1, Prague 1 (next to the historic National Theatre building), tel 224 901 448; Ovocný trh 6. Prague 1 (Kolowrat Theatre building), tel 224 901 448

• State Opera box office: Wilsonova 4, Prague 1, tel 224 227 266

• Obecní dům: Náměstí Republiky 5, Prague 1, tel 222 002 100

• Rudolfinum: Alšovo nábřeží 12, Prague 1, tel 227 059 227

• Ticketpro: Lucerna arcade, Štěpanská 61,

Prague 1, tel 224 818 080; GTS Alive, Letenská 1, Prague 1, tel 226 222 333
• Ticketstream: CK Čedok, Rytířská 16, Prague 1, tel 224 227 723; CK Čedok Na Příkopě 18, Prague 1, tel 224 197 615
• Bontonland: Palác Koruna, Wenceslas Square 1, Prague 1, tel 224 473 080
• Sazka Ticket: Lucerna arcade, Štěpanská 61, Prague 1, tel 266 121 122

Tour guides
There are many tour services available in Prague; your choice will depend on location, language and cost. The concierge at your hotel is usually a useful place to start, although the PIS desk in Old Town Hall can also provide helpful suggestions, as well as tour guides for hire in several languages. Suggested tour services you can find yourself include:
• Prague Sightseeing Tours/Cityrama: Klimentská 52/176, tel 222 230 208
• Premiant City Tour: Na Příkopě 23, tel 606 600 123

If you walk down Na Příkopě between Wenceslas Square and Náměstí Republiky, you will see a number of kiosks offering tours. Most of these offer trips to interesting destinations outside Prague, such as Karlovy Vary, Kutná Hora, Česky Krumlov and Karlštejn.

Boat trips
Many cruise boats ply the Vltava River, some offering basic sightseeing tours, others with drinking and dining services and live music. Most depart from the quay next to the Čechův bridge (Čechův most), which is at the north end of Pařižska street in Old Town (Pařižska starts in Old Town Square and runs north through Josefov). You can check timetables and tour options at the dock.

Prague card
PIS sells a Prague Tourist Card that offers free or reduced admission to more than 50

EMERGENCY INFORMATION

Ambulance 155
Police 158
Fire 150
General emergency 112
Emergency road service 1230/ 1240

Dental emergencies
Nemocnice Na Františku, Palackého 5, Prague 1, tel 224 946 981
European Dental Centre, Wenceslas Square 33, Prague 1, tel 224 228 984/ 224 228 994

Hospitals and clinics
Motol Hospital, V Úvalu 84, Prague 5, tel 224 431 111
Health Care Centre Národní, Národní 9, Prague 1, tel 222 075 120
Na Homolce, Roentgenova 2, Prague 5, tel 257 271 111
Canadian Medical Care, Veleslavínská 1/30, Prague 6, tel 235 360 133

24-hour pharmacies
Palackého 5, Prague 1, tel 224 946 982
Belgická 37, Prague 2, tel 222 519 731
Stefánikova 6, Prague 5, tel 257 320 918
Vltězné náměstí 13, Prague 6, tel 224 326 210

---

museums and other attractions, including Prague Castle, for four days. As this book went to press, the cost was 790 Kč for adults and 530 Kč for students. For a full list of attractions and other information, see www.praguecitycard.com.

Lost property
There is a lost-and-found office at Karoliny Svetlé 5 in Prague 1 (tel 224 235 085), but quite honestly, don't bother. This is a country with a high rate of theft, which is why all the shopkeepers watch you suspiciously from the minute you walk in

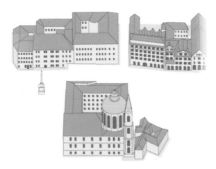

their door. If you've lost or had something stolen, it's gone, no matter how dear or precious it was. Keep track of your packages and valuables, and don't ever put something down and look away, or trust it will be there when you come back from the bathroom.

If you have travel insurance and want to file a claim for lost or stolen property, keep in mind that you will you need a 'protocol' from the Prague police confirming your loss. Contact your embassy to find out which police station has staff that speak your language.

If you have left an item on the metro or a tram or bus, call the Public Transport Hotline (800 191 817) immediately. A dispatcher will try to contact the driver and have him look for it.

For lost credit cards, call the following numbers:
• American Express: 222 800 222
• Visa, MasterCard and Eurocard: 272 771 111
• Diners Club: 267 197 450

Opening hours
Most **major attractions** are open from 9 or 10am to 5 or 6pm. Almost all the **museums** are closed on Mondays. Most attractions change their hours of operation during the off-season (generally October to April). Hours at the major **churches** vary.

Most **banks** are open from 9am to 5pm. **Shops** are generally open from 9 or 10am to 5 or 6pm on weekdays, and 9am to noon or

1pm on Saturdays. Most of the shops in the main tourist areas in the city centre stay open until 9pm or later Mondays to Saturdays, and 6pm on Sundays.

Once you get out of the city centre, do not expect anything to be open on weekends except for **restaurants** and **grocery stores**. Also, keep in mind that just because certain hours are posted on a shop door or website, that doesn't mean they will necessarily be observed.

Most **supermarkets** open at 8 or 9am and close at 7 or 8pm, with shorter hours on Sundays.

The opening hours for **pubs, cafés** and **restaurants** tend to vary widely. Keep in mind that Prague is not a late-night dining town. So if you're looking for food after 10pm, your options will be limited mostly to sausage and pizza stands, or fast-food restaurants. Most **pubs** stop serving alcohol at 11pm.

Public holidays
1 January
Easter Monday
1 May Labour Day
8 May Liberation Day – 1945
5 July Sts Cyril and Methodius Day
6 July Jan Hus Day
28 September Czech Statehood Day
28 October Independent Czechoslovak State Proclamation Day (1918)
17 November Day of Struggle for Liberty and Democracy
24 December Christmas Eve
25 December Christmas Day
26 December St Stephen's Day

Introducing Prague on Foot

This walk offers a quick introduction to the city. It's a useful way to get your bearings or, if you have only a day to see Prague, to take in many of the highlights, which you can go back and explore in more detail another time. The main part of the walk takes you along what is known as the Royal Way, the coronation route that Czech kings from the 15th to 19th centuries strode from the Powder Tower, which marks the traditional seat of Czech royalty, to Prague Castle. Because the city also has a modern face that is an indelible part of its character, we start at a significant 20thC departure point, the top (southeast end) of Wenceslas Square.

Standing in front of the **National Museum**, you can take in a sweeping vista of **Wenceslas Square**, where huge crowds gathered for all the most important events of the 20th century: the founding of the Czechoslovak Republic in 1918, the invasion of Nazi troops in 1939, the crushing of Prague Spring in 1968 and the Velvet Revolution in 1989, when the entire world watched throngs celebrate their new freedom. Walking down the centre of the Square will give you a better look at the stunning architecture that lines both sides of the street, and, unfortunately, the enormous billboards that increasingly cover it.

The Square ends at the T-shaped intersection of **Října** (on your left), **Na Můstku** (straight ahead) and **Na Příkopě** (to your right). Turn right on to Na Příkopě, known as Prague's 'high street' for its sparkling collection of shops, malls and high-end offices and restaurants. Recently, Pařížská street in Old Town has become the preferred location for the city's most exclusive shops. But Na Příkopě offers unique gems, such as the Museum of Communism sitting atop a McDonald's.

Na Příkopě ends at **Náměstí Republiky**, which has taken on a modern look with the renovated **Hybernia Theatre** and massive **Palladium mall**. But the first thing you will see, on your left, is the imposing **Powder Tower**, a blackened masterpiece of Gothic architecture. It's attached to the **Municipal House (Obecní dům)**, a multi-purpose facility built in the early 1900s as a breathtaking monument to the glories of Art Nouveau.

Turn left and walk under the Powder Tower, and you're following in the footsteps of kings on the **Royal Way**. The route proceeds along **Celetná street**, which is now a monument to the tourist trade, packed with hotels, restaurants and souvenir shops.

Celetná brings you to **Old Town Square**, the heart of historic Prague. You could spend hours exploring the museums and monuments here, but a quick glance around will reveal many of the square's most interesting features: the towering twin-spired church of **Our Lady Before Týn**, where Tycho Brahe is buried; the **monument** to the religious martyr Jan Hus in the middle of the Square; **St Nicholas Church**, the domed Baroque masterpiece on the northwest corner; and **Old Town Hall**, with the world-famous **Astronomical Clock** on its southern face.

Walk past Old Town Hall with the Astronomical Clock on your right, and you will quickly come to a small square, **Malé náměstí**. Continue straight through the square, and at the other end take the quick zigzag through **Jilská** (there's no other way to go), then the first street on your right, **Kárlova**. This will take you to the **Charles Bridge**. Along the way you'll pass a raucous array of souvenir shops and the enormous **Clementinum**, the Jesuit enclave where Johannes Kepler made astronomical observations.

Kárlova ends at the Charles Bridge. The towers that anchor both ends are some of the

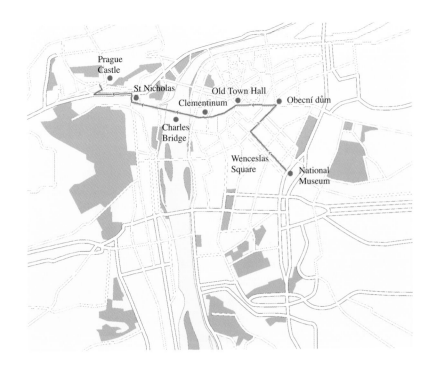

oldest of their type in Europe, and in between is a wealth of interesting statuary – not to mention some splendid views of **Prague Castle**. Crossing the bridge over the Vltava River puts you in **Malá Strana**, Prague's 'lesser quarter'.

As the Charles Bridge ends it will drop you naturally on **Mostecká street**. Follow this straight for a few blocks until it opens into **Malostranské náměstí**, which wraps around the domed St Nicholas Church. For the best quick view of it, stay left when you come into the square, cross **Karmelitská** (look left for speeding trams coming through a blind turn) and walk under the colonnade to the back part of the square. There you will see the entrance to St Nicholas and, in the middle of the square, a **plague column**. Walk past the column and turn left on to the street that goes uphill.

This is **Nerudova**, the last leg of the Royal Way, lined with well-preserved historical buildings and a charming mix of shops, pubs and restaurants. Look to your right for a wide stone staircase, which after a few steps splits left and right. Take the stairs on your right, and within moments you will be at Prague Castle. This being the 21st century, there's no crown awaiting you. But you will be rewarded for your efforts with a grand view over the city.

If you have the time to spend, Prague Castle and its adjoining grounds and gardens are well worth exploring. An additional 15 minutes would be enough for a quick look inside **St Vitus**, the largest Gothic cathedral in Eastern Europe. If this marks the end of your walk, you have two options for returning to the city centre, both on the no. 22 tram. Turn your back to the Castle gates and walk out of the square, keeping the small triangular park on your right. This will put you on **Loretánská street**, which intersects after about four blocks with **Keplerova**, where you will see the **Pohořelec** tram stop. Or go into the Castle gates, through the first courtyard and into the second courtyard, where you will see an archway exit on your left. Go through the archway, across the bridge and past the **Riding School Gallery** to **Mariánské Hradby**, a busy street where you will see the **Pražsky hrad** tram stop.

The Jewish Quarter: Josefov

This neighbourhood is the site of one of the oldest Jewish ghettos in Europe, dating back to at least the 11th century, though it's hard to imagine now, as you stroll past its glitzy shops and bustling cafés. Josefov has been the setting for persecution, pogroms, a massive fire that wiped out more than 300 buildings and a late-19thC razing that left only the cemetery, town hall and six synagogues standing.

Ironically, Adolf Hitler is responsible for much of what can be seen today. Instead of destroying the Jewish Quarter, he intended to preserve it as a living museum, housing the final artefacts of the race he planned to exterminate.

Josefov also gave birth to one of the great myths of Central Europe: the Golem. It was here that Rabbi Löw breathed life into the giant creature made, as the story goes, of mud and clay, who patrolled the streets at night, protecting the inhabitants of the Jewish Quarter. When the Golem ran amok, the rabbi banished it to the attic of the Old New Synagogue, where according to folklore it remains. But the idea never died, inspiring many other incarnations over the centuries, including the most famous, the Frankenstein monster.

Today, the focus in Josefov is on the preservation of Jewish history and on tributes to Prague's esteemed literary son, Franz Kafka, which you'll find scattered through the neighbourhood.

STARTS

Look out for fascinating architectural details amidst the more ordinary shops and houses.

▶ **STARTS**
The Rudolfinum.
Nearest metro stop:
Staroměstská.

■ **ENDS**
Old Town Square.
Nearest metro stop:
Staroměstská.

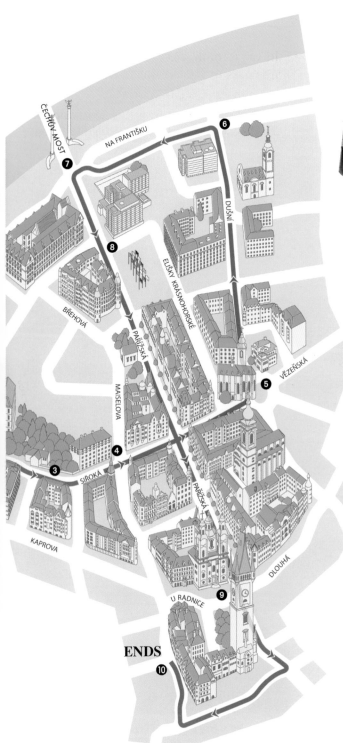

PRAGUE

*Homages to Franz
Kafka, Prague's most
esteemed literary son,
are found throughout
the city.*

ENDS

19

The imposing Rudolfinum.

❶ The **Rudolfinum**, Prague's premier concert hall, was built in the late 1800s in the neo-Classical style. The building has also served as home to the Czechoslovak parliament, and it was headquarters for Reichsprotektor Reinhard Heydrich during the Nazi occupation. According to a local story, which may or may not be true, Heydrich was furious to learn that Felix Mendelssohn was among the composers whose statues ring the roof of the building, and ordered it taken down. Unsure of which statue portrayed Mendelssohn, a Jew, workers removed the one with the biggest nose. None of that unpleasantness is in evidence today. Instead, the Rudolfinum houses two superb concert halls - the large Dvořák Hall for orchestra concerts, and smaller Suk Hall for chamber music - and one of the finest art galleries in the city.

❷ With the Rudolfinum to your left and the river behind you, cross **Križnovická** and enter **Josefov** on **Široká street**. The large building on your left opposite the Rudolfinum is the **Museum of Decorative Arts**, a handsome neo-Renaissance structure with an impressive collection of furniture, tapestries, clocks and the like, as well as rotating shows by local artists. The wall that suddenly appears along Široká encircles the **Old Jewish Cemetery**, which for hundreds of years was the only place in Prague where Jews could be buried. As a result, bodies are stacked on bodies, and tombstones jut out and collide in a riot of odd angles.

❸ Continue briefly along Široká to the **Pinkas Synagogue**, one of the entry points for the **Jewish Museum complex**, which comprises four synagogues, the Ceremonial Hall and the Old Jewish Cemetery. Like many of the shops and restaurants in the neighbourhood, the entrance fee is comparatively expensive, so, if you are travelling on a budget, you may want to consider whether your time and money would be better spent elsewhere. Inside the synagogue, the first version of which was built on the site in 1535, you'll find a memorial to the Holocaust victims of Bohemia and Moravia, with more than 80,000 names painstakingly engraved on the walls.

Antonin Dvořák.

The Museum of Decorative Arts.

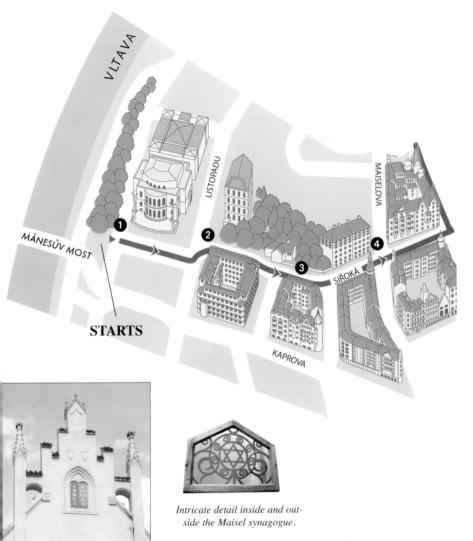

STARTS

Intricate detail inside and outside the Maisel synagogue.

❹ Turning left out the Synagogue, continue along Široká to reach **Maiselova**, where a brief detour to the right will bring you to the **Maisel Synagogue**. Named after the mayor of the Jewish Quarter during the reign of Rudolf II, it was said to be the most sumptuous synagogue in Prague until it burned down in the great fire of 1689. The current neo-Gothic structure houses an exhibition tracing the history of the Jewish people in Bohemia and Moravia. Back on Široká, look for the **Franz Kafka Café** on your right, a cosy spot to stop for cake and coffee or a beer. Continue another three blocks along Široká.

Kafka finds his way into every aspect of the city.

21

THE JEWISH QUARTER: JOSEFOV

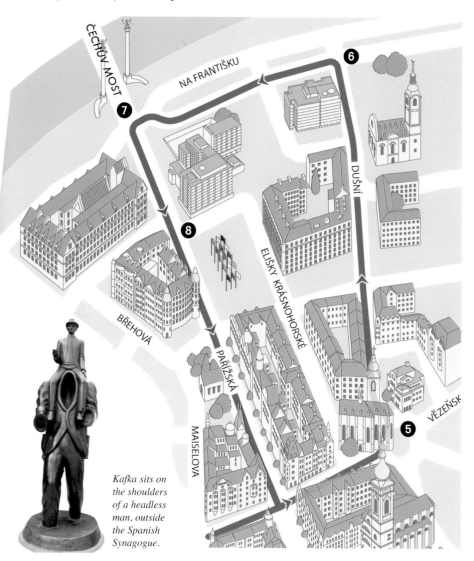

Kafka sits on the shoulders of a headless man, outside the Spanish Synagogue.

❺ The **Spanish Synagogue** sits on a small square with a number of interesting features. The synagogue on the north side is unimposing, and gives no hint of the eye-popping interior. Every inch of the ceiling and wall is covered in elaborate patterns and floral designs, a style taken from the 14thC Moorish Alhambra at Grenada, Spain. If you get a chance to attend a concert there during your visit, it's worth it for the atmosphere alone. Outside the synagogue is one of the many memorials to Franz Kafka, and easily the most puzzling: the author sits on the shoulders of a much larger, headless man. The sculptor, Jaroslav Rona, has never explained the meaning behind this.

Across the street are two good dining options: **Kolkovna**, a boisterous restaurant that serves hearty Czech food and beer, and **Nostress Café**, which offers lighter fare in a modish setting.

6 Head north out of the square along **Dušni**, and in a few minutes look out for the mammoth **Sts Simon and Jude Church**. Originally built between 1615 and 1620, the church was rebuilt in the 18th century with an impressive Baroque façade. This is another concert venue worth visiting. The acoustics are excellent, and the altar features a monumental *trompe l'oeil* portrayal of heaven and earth by the noted mural artist Václav Vavřinec Rainel. Both Mozart and Haydn have supposedly played the organ in this church.

An ornate shop on Pařižká.

7 Turning right out of the church, you reach the river, where a left turn and brief walk will bring you to the **Čechův bridge**, with its distinctive torch bearer columns. Across the river sits a curious object at the top of the hill: a **giant metronome**, which operates only on the rare occasions some public-minded company is willing to pay for the electricity to run it. No current Prague resident seems able to explain exactly why it was built, although everyone (whether they're old enough or not) remembers what stood there before it - the world's largest statue of Josef Stalin, a 50-metre tall, 17,000-ton behemoth that portrayed the Soviet dictator leading a band of loyal proletarians. Its creator, Otakar Švec, committed suicide the day after it was unveiled on May 1, 1955. When it was finally destroyed in 1962, it took 800 kilograms of explosive to bring it down.

One of the columns of Čechův bridge.

8 Take the immediate left off **Dvořáko** and head down **Pařižká**. Stalin could never have imagined that the street he was overlooking, Pařižká, would one day be a monument to capitalism. Stroll the tree-lined boulevard to Old Town Square and you'll see that it is exactly that, lined with names such as Versace, Giorgio Armani, Hermés, Dior, Cartier and Swarovski. As a rule of thumb, you don't want to make high-end purchases in Prague, where the prices for designer clothing and jewellery tend to be higher than in other European cities. But this is the best street in the city to window shop, with many pleasant street cafés along the way. As you continue down Pařižká, look out on your right for the **Old New Synagogue** (or more accurately, the back of it), the traditional centre of Prague's Jewish community and, by some accounts, the oldest active synagogue in Europe. If you take a short detour down the alley that runs next to it, you can pop into the High Synagogue Gift Shop.

Old New Synagogue.

23

9 Keep walking down Pařížká for around three blocks until you reach **Old Town Square**. The massive church on your right as you enter the square is **St Nicholas**, which has served many functions over the course of its 400-year history: a Roman Catholic church, a storage warehouse, a Russian Orthodox church and, currently, a concert hall. The

St Nicholas Church.

Baroque structure, with its distinctive dome and twin spires, was built between 1653 and 1755. The mural inside the dome depicts scenes from the life of St Benedict (the church was once attached to a Benedictine monastery), though it's hard to see in any detail. More accessible are the expressive sandstone sculptures on the southern face of the building, done by Antonín Braun as part of the original construction. Perhaps the most impressive thing about St Nicholas is that, while other churches were allowed to decay, this one was restored during the 1950s by the communists. They kept their reasons to themselves, but the tower reportedly made a great spy roost for the secret police.

10 This neighbourhood was the boyhood hangout of Franz Kafka, who went to primary school a few blocks away on Masná, and whose father had a shop on the north-east corner of what is now Old Town Square. Just past St Nicholas, a small **museum** with a Kafka exhibition and souvenirs marks the author's birthplace. However, this is not the place for serious Kafka fans. If you want to learn more about his work and life in Prague, visit the Kafka Museum across the river (Cihelná 2b in Mála Strana), or consider an excursion to the Žižkov neighbourhood to visit his grave in the New Jewish Cemetery.

This square was also the site of executions during the medieval era, when serious offenders were dispatched with a public beheading. If you're facing the Kafka Museum and turn completely around, you will see the pub **U Kata** ('at the execution site') with its skull-and-crossbones-style logo of an executioner's head and crossed axes. Stop for a beer and consider your good fortune to have been born in the 20th century. Or walk up **Karpova** street to return to your starting point at the Rudolfinum.

Kafka's boyhood hangout now bears his name.

Enjoy a drink 'at the execution site'.

Origins of a City: Charles Bridge to Old Town Square

E very European city worth visiting has an historic centre, but none quite like Prague's Old Town. It was the city's good fortune not to be overrun, bombed or burned during the major wars of the 20th century, leaving ten centuries of art and architecture intact. Parts of Old Town were razed and reconstructed, particularly at the end of the 19th and beginning of the 20th centuries, so the juxtaposition of medieval and modern can sometimes be jarring. But the aesthetics are uniformly fascinating, and this being the Czech Republic, you are never more than a few steps from a tasty Czech beer.

The original settlements in Old Town date back to the first half of the 10th century, with Old Town Square always at the hub as a busy market-place. The Judith Bridge, the first bridge across the Vltava linking Old Town with Malá Strana, was built in 1172. It was the only stone bridge in Europe at the time, washed away in a 1342 flood and replaced by the Charles Bridge. Old Town got its own town hall in 1338, Charles IV established a

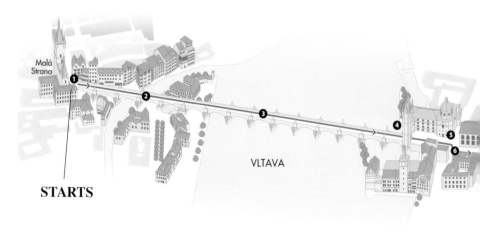

Malá Strana

VLTAVA

STARTS

View over Prague from Charles Bridge.

One of the many statues lining Charles Bridge.

university there in 1438, and over the next century it was among the pre-eminent royal towns of Central Europe. As other boroughs were grafted on to form the city, it diminished in importance but remained the natural centre of Prague, as it is today.

Capitalism may still be only a rumour on the outreaches of the city, but it caught on quickly in Old Town, whose historic streets are lined with garish souvenir shops, most selling exactly the same items. This is most evident along what is known as the Royal Way, the coronation route that kings rode from the Powder Tower at náměstí Republiky to Prague Castle. But there's plenty to explore along less-travelled side-streets. And if you see an intriguing lane or alleyway, follow it. Getting lost in the medieval maze is half the fun of exploring Old Town.

▶ **STARTS**
Malá Strana. Nearest metro stop: Malostranská.

■ **ENDS**
Finish: Old Town Square. Nearest metro stop: Staromětska.

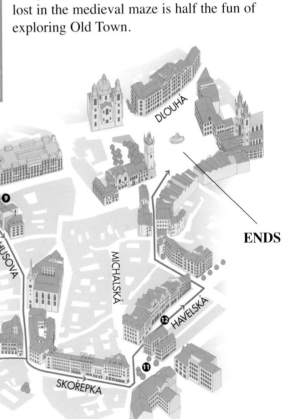

ENDS

St Roch, and the dog who cured him of the plague, adorn a building in Liliova.

Origins of a City: Charles Bridge to Old Town Square

The mismatched towers.

❶ Your approach to Old Town starts at the western end of **Charles Bridge**, in **Malá Strana**. The two towers there frame a Gothic archway dating from 1411, erected on an even older Roman construction site. The smaller tower is part of the original **Judith Bridge**, now attached to a 16th century Renaissance building that was once a toll house. The taller of the towers was built in 1464 to mirror the more elaborate tower on the western end of the bridge. The eastern face of the connecting walkway features carved stone symbols of the Bohemian nations (Bohemia, Moravia and Lower Lusatia) and, below, emblems of Old Town and Malá Strana.

Detail from the western tower.

❷ Unless you are there late at night or very early on a winter morning, there is no way to avoid the crowds on Charles Bridge, Prague's single biggest tourist attraction. Along with mobs of tourists, it attracts vendors, sketch artists, buskers, beggars and pickpockets – so pay attention. The bridge took nearly 50 years to build from the time it was started in 1357, and is a remarkable structure for its time: 516 m long and nearly 10 m wide, with 16 arches. The statues were added beginning in the early 1700s, with the thirtieth and final one (Sts Cyril and Methodius, eleventh on the left as you walk toward Old Town) put in place in 1938. Most of the ones you see today are copies of the originals, long ago degraded.

The view from Charles Bridge.

Statue of St Francis.

❸ Almost every statue on the bridge is noteworthy in some respect, and sadly space restricts us to mention only two of the most interesting. **St John Nepomuk** (eighth on the left) has two golden plaques at its base. According to legend, if you touch the one on the right, which shows him being thrown into the river, and make a wish, it will come true. The sculpture of the **Holy Cross** (thirteenth on the left) has a strikingly odd combination of faiths, a Christian crucifix topped by a Hebrew inscription that translates as 'Holy, holy, holy Lord of the masses'. The inscription was supposedly paid for by a Jew who was fined for mocking the cross. In the summer of 2007, after a 650th birthday party for the bridge, major renovation work began on it that is expected to last for at least a decade.

The worn golden plaque under the statue of St John Nepomuk.

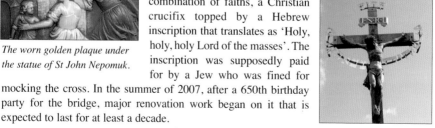

The Holy Cross.

[Read less](/)

PRAGUE

Left, the highly-ornamented eastern tower. Above, painted detail from its ceiling.

❹ The **Old Town Bridge Tower** on the eastern end of the bridge was originally part of the fortifications for Old Town. Completed in the early 1400s, it is still considered one of the most beautiful bridge towers in Europe, covered with elaborate ornamental work and Gothic sculptures of Czech kings and saints. (The sculptures on the western side of the tower were destroyed in the Swedish siege of 1648.) The vault in the passage way is modelled after the presbytery in St Vitus Cathedral, and covered with murals originally painted in the late 14th century. This tower has a notorious history. For a time, it was a debtors' prison. And in 1621, the heads of a dozen Czech leaders of the Estates uprising against the Habsburgs were hung from the spire as a warning to other would-be rebels.

❺ Before you cross busy **Křižovnická** to formally enter Old Town, you will see the **Church of St Francis Seraph** on the left, established in 1679 by a religious order known as the Red Star Crusaders. The interior of the distinctive dome is covered with a swirling mural of The Last Judgment, and an underground portion of the church features elements of the original Gothic structure. Directly across the street is the **Church of the Holy Saviour**, which is part of the Clementinum complex. Its grimy Baroque façade is populated by statues of famous saints, topped by Christ the Redeemer, who is flanked by the four apostles of the gospels: from left to right, Luke, John, Matthew and Mark.

Church of St Francis.

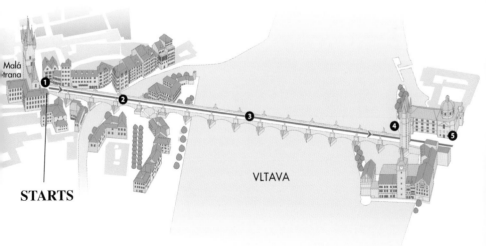

Malá Strana

VLTAVA

STARTS

6 As you walk along **Karlova**, which is part of the original **Royal Way**, you will see a plaque at the address **188/4**, the house where Johannes Kepler lived when he wrote his revolutionary *Astronomia Nova*, which established the laws of planetary motion. The street is quite narrow until it opens into a small square at **Liliova**, where a gold snake emblem adorns **U zlatého hada** (At the Golden Snake), said to be the first café established in Prague. At the other end of the square, **U zlaté studně** (At the Golden Well) is a former apothecary that dispensed medicine. The two lowest relief figures on the face of the building are Sts Sebastian (left) and Roch, known for healing plague victims. St Roch was himself a victim of the plague, and is always pictured with a dog, which according to legend befriended him during his illness and licked his wounds clean.

Clockwise from top: Johannes Kepler's house; the house 'At the Golden Well'; and the cafe 'At the Golden Snake'.

7 A left turn through the archway in the north wall of the square will take you into the sprawling **Clementinum**, which occupies an entire large city block. Originally a much smaller Dominican monastery, it was taken over in the mid-17th century by the Jesuits, who expanded it over the next hundred years to include churches, schools, libraries, a theatre and a printing house built around five courtyards. The astronomical tower in the centre was reportedly used by Kepler for star gazing. Until the 1920s, it was also used to calculate the time: at high noon every day, when the sun crossed a

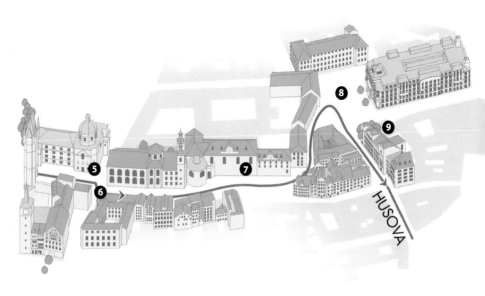

certain point, an observer in the tower signalled the castle and a cannon was fired. Only a small portion of the complex is open to the public, but the **Baroque Library Hall** and **Astronomical Tower** are worth seeing, as are the chamber music concerts regularly held in the splendiferous **Mirror Chapel**. You will pass the entrance for all three as you walk north through two courtyards, leaving to your right through the arched passage way in the second one.

Inside the Clementinum complex.

Prague City Library.

❽ The passage way brings you out on **Mariánské náměstí**, which is dominated by two large buidings. The modern one to your left (on the north side of the square) is **Prague City Library**. Directly across from the Clementinum, on the east side of the square, is **Prague City Hall**, which boasts two distinctive statues on its street-level flanks. The one on the right (as you face the building) is Rabbi Löw, the legendary creator of the Golem. The Darth Vader lookalike on the left is the Iron Knight, a tragic figure who returned from the wars and abandoned his betrothed when he was told she had been unfaithful. In despair, both she and her father killed themselves. As a result, the knight is cursed. His statue is said to come to life every 100 years, doomed to walk the streets and repeat the cycle endlessly until he can find a virgin who will spend an hour with him.

Above, the tragic Iron Knight. Top, Rabbi Löw.

The warriors of Clam-Gallas.

❾ Leaving the square via **Husova**, on the south side, takes you past monumental **Clam-Gallas Palace**, an 18th century High Baroque behemoth with fierce warriors eternally struggling to hold up the doorway pediments. Used primarily for exhibitions and tourist concerts now, Clam-Gallas lays claim to two noteworthy musical performances: one by Mozart in 1787, and the other by Beethoven nine years later. After you cross **Karlova**, the towering **Church of St Giles** looms on your left. Founded in 1371, the church has been rebuilt many times since, with its patchwork architectural history evident on the south side of the building, where one of the original Gothic doorways sits next to a Baroque doorway from the 1730s. You will know you've reached the end of Husova when you see a man dangling precariously from a plank atop a building. The sculpture is by David Černý, the art prankster responsible for the inverted St Wenceslas statue in Lucerna and the peeing statues outside the Kafka Museum.

Left and above left: detail on buildings along Husova. Right, one of David Černý's unorthodox sculptures.

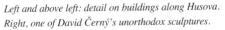

The fountain scultpure
in Uhelný trh.

HUSOVA

DLOUHÁ

ENDS

MICHALSKÁ

HAVELSKÁ

⑫

⑪

⑩

SKOŘEPKA

⑩ A brief detour to the right takes you to **Betlémské
náměstí**, the site of **Bethlehem Chapel**. First built in the late
14th century and reconstructed in the 1950s, this church is
noteworthy chiefly as the place where Jan Hus preached from
1402 to 1413, to standing-room only crowds. After advocating

Betlémské náměstí.

reforms that anticipated Martin Luther by 100 years, Hus was declared a heretic, excommunicated by the Catholic Church in 1411 and burned at the stake in 1415. But he had a large and devoted following, which was responsible for the first Prague defenestration at New Town Hall in 1419, and a few months later launched the Hussite wars, which lasted for nearly 14 years. Hus remains a martyr and beloved figure in Bohemia, with his memorial statue the centrepiece of Old Town Square.

① Retrace your steps and cross Husova to follow **Skořepka street** to **Uhelný trh**, a small square that was once a coal market. The fountain sculpture is a copy of the original, created in 1797. The hotel and restaurant prominently marked **Wolfgang** is one of the places Mozart stayed in Prague, though not for

Decorated house along Skořepka.

long – the coal market was so noisy that he couldn't work, and fled in search of quiet. Franz Liszt had better luck at the adjacent **Platýz house**, where he gave performances late in his career.

Mozart spent a few disturbed nights here.

② Cross the square to **Havelská**, the site of a street market that offers a charming, if odd, mix of souvenirs and produce. The latter is mostly on display during the week, when local residents walk by the market on their way to work to pick up fresh fruit and vegetables – which, if you're interested, are usually cheaper later in the day. On

Uhelný trh.

weekends, the stalls are given over to souvenir dealers, and if you need to pick up some items to take home, this is a good place to do it. There's a better selection than you'll find in most of the souvenir shops, and many of the vendors are willing to barter. The market ends at **Melantrichova**, where a left turn and several blocks' walk brings you to **Old Town Square**.

Top left and left, colourful stalls along Havelská. Right, Melantrichova.

Old Town Walk: Old Town Square to Obecní dům

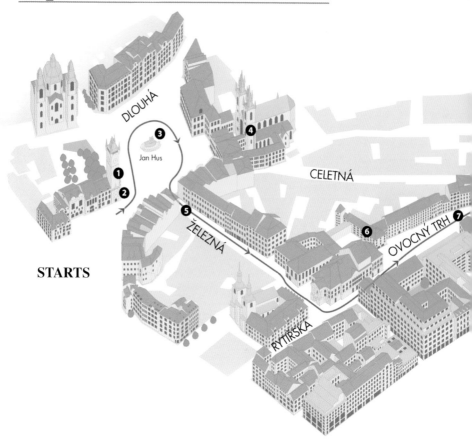

No single place better embodies Prague past and present than Old Town Square, where throngs of tourists gather to watch the famed astronomical clock strike the hour, as it has for centuries, then repair to glitzy modern restaurants to eat overpriced Czech goulash and *vepřové a knedlíky* (pork and dumplings). For sheer spectacle, there's no better place in the city, especially in the summer, when everything from jazz concerts to marathon races are held on the Square. It's also the centre of the Christmas holiday season, with long rows of colourful vendors' booths set up around a towering Christmas tree and the sweet smell of mulled wine wafting through the air.

The tourist guides don't usually talk about the darker side of the Square, which is indicated by the four small spires ringing the major spires on Tyn church – the sign of an execution site. Hussite heads rolled here

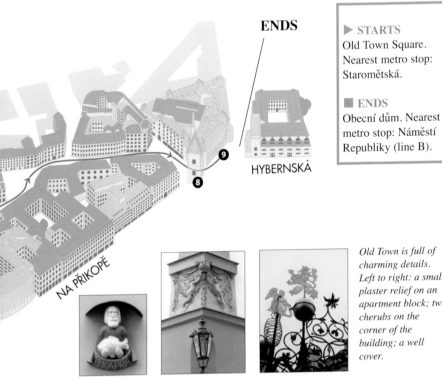

ENDS

▶ **STARTS**
Old Town Square.
Nearest metro stop:
Staroměstská.

■ **ENDS**
Obecní dům. Nearest
metro stop: Náměstí
Republiky (line B).

HYBERNSKÁ

NA PŘÍKOPĚ

Old Town is full of charming details. Left to right: a small plaster relief on an apartment block; two cherubs on the corner of the building; a well cover.

during the 1420s and 30s, and in 1621, after a failed revolt against the Habsburgs, 27 Czech knights and noblemen lost their heads (a dozen of which were hung from the Old Town Bridge Tower). The Square was the scene of brief but violent fighting in the waning days of the Second World War, followed by a massive celebration when the Russian army finally liberated the city on May 9, 1945. By agreement, the Americans stopped in Pilseň and let the Russians march triumphant into Prague, which became a major factor in the country's decision to turn communist three years later, announced to cheering crowds on Old Town Square.

Now, the largest and most enthusiastic crowds on the Square are likely to be there for sporting events, such as the big-screen broadcast of the winter Olympics from Nagano in 1998, when the Czech ice hockey team took the gold medal. The Square is also a magnet for marauding groups of drunken tourists, especially British stag parties. Find a comfortable seat and something to drink and take it all in: you are literally at the crossroads of Central Europe.

Old Town Square.

1 **Old Town Hall** dominates the west side of the Square, boasting a 70 m tower with the **astronomical clock** at its base. The original structure dates from 1338, though what stands now is only part of what was cobbled together over the intervening centuries, with entire wings destroyed by Nazi troops as they tried to hold the city in the final days of the Second World War. Today the building houses a **tourist information** service, exhibitions and the most popular wedding hall in Prague. The view from the tower is well worth the climb, but many of the most interesting features are on the outside, starting with the astronomical clock. The peaked gable on the eastern face is an oriel chapel window, and the elaborate *sgraffito* on the western side covers what is known as the 'House of One Minute', which dates from 1610.

Old Town Hall.

Five figures flank an ornate window in Old Town Hall.

2 The first version of the remarkable astronomical clock started ticking in 1410, and has stopped only for repairs and improvements since. Every hour on the hour between 8 am and 8 pm, the twelve apostles and four allegorical figures – greed, vanity, death and the Turk – come to life in what is touted as a mini-morality play. There's not much to it, leaving many visitors disappointed. Of more enduring interest is the complex upper face of the clock, which tracks the movement of the moon and the planets through the zodiac and displays three different measures of time: 24-hour Central European time, stellar time (the hours of daylight) and Old Bohemian time (which runs backward, starting at sunset). Sharp eyes will pick up the clock's medieval origins in the sun, positioned at the tip of one hand, revolving around the earth at the centre.

The astronomical clock.

Above and right: two more regally decorated windows.

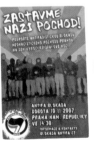

Left and above: colourful posters advertise events the guidebooks don't mention.

Baroque splendour in the Square.

3 **Jan Hus** stands in the middle of Old Town Square, an unlikely national hero in what is now a largely atheist country. Religion was beaten out of the Czechs during half a century of Nazi and communist occupation, but its vestiges are still central to the culture, with churches rivalled only by castles as the showpieces of the country, and a national holiday devoted to Sts Cyril and Methodius, missionaries who brought Christianity and the printed word to the Czech lands. The Hus memorial is ringed by rows of beautifully restored Baroque and Gothic buildings, each a story in itself. Of particular interest are **Kinský Palace** and the **House at the Stone Bell** on the east side of the Square, now fine museums operated by the National Gallery. If you look closely at the buildings on the south side of the Square, you'll find plaques commemorating the places where composer Bedřich Smetana ran a music school (**no. 20**) and Albert Einstein met friends for coffee (**no. 17**).

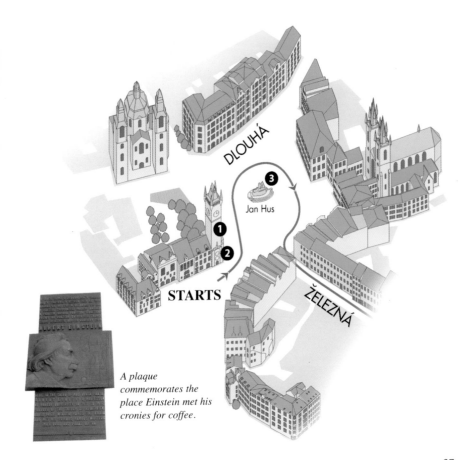

DLOUHÁ

3 Jan Hus

1

2

STARTS

ŽELEZNÁ

A plaque commemorates the place Einstein met his cronies for coffee.

The spires of Our Lady Before Týn.

❹ The twin spires of **Our Lady Before Týn church** arose in the late 15th and early 16th centuries, and have housed several different denominations, including Hussites, Calixtines and Catholics. When the Jesuits took over the church in the 17th century, they had the golden chalice on the front, a Hussite symbol, removed, melted down and recast as the Madonna and Child relief now mounted on the gable of the frontispiece. The Jesuits are also responsible for the rich Baroque interior, which preserved some of the existing Gothic elements, like the Calvary Altar at the front of the northern aisle.

A number of famous people are interred at Our Lady Before Týn, most notably Tycho Brahe, the Danish astronomer who worked in the court of Rudolf II. His tombstone is located at the column nearest the altar on the south side of the church.

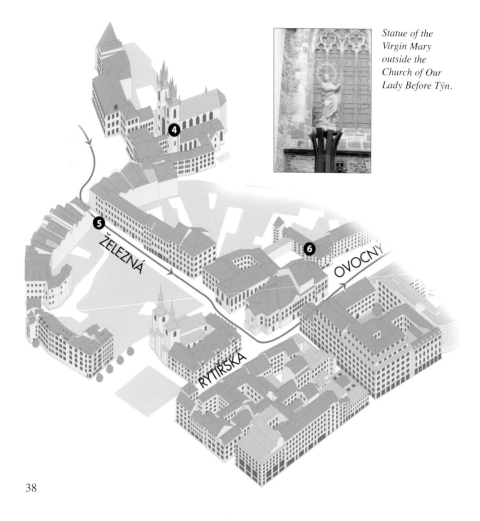

Statue of the Virgin Mary outside the Church of Our Lady Before Týn.

5 The tourist flow out of Old Town Square runs east along **Celetná**, which is part of the old **Royal Way**, lined now with handsome restored buildings and souvenir shops. Culturally, a better alternative is to take **Železná**, which runs south out of the Square to the neo-classical **Estates Theatre**. After opening as the Count Nostitz theatre in 1783, this quickly became the centre of Prague's love affair with Mozart. After a wildly successful run of *The Marriage of Figaro* at the theatre in 1786, Mozart visited Prague twice in 1787. On his first visit in January, he conducted his *Prague Symphony in D major* and *The Marriage of Figaro* at the theatre, and accepted a commission to compose and return with a new opera. This was *Don Giovanni*, which he premiered at the Nostitz Theatre on October 29, 1787. A sculpture at the front entrance by Anna Chromy, depicting the ghost of the slain *commendatore*, commemorates the occasion.

Železná.

6 The building directly to the north of the Estates Theatre (left as you're facing the theatre) is the **Carolinum**, the university established in Old Town by Charles IV in 1348. Now part of the city-wide Charles University complex, it was extensively refurbished during the 1950s and 60s, producing a handsome work of modern international architecture that retains some of the Gothic and Baroque elements. Architecturally, its most interesting feature is the restored Gothic bay window that faces the theatre, decorated with gargoyles, coats of arms and other ornamental stonework.

The Estates Theatre.

Anna Chromy's Il Commendatore.

The Carolinum's Gothic bay window.

An intriguing shop on Železná.

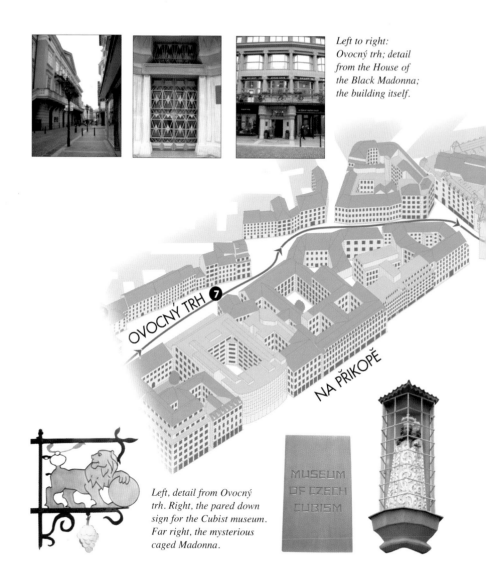

*Left to right:
Ovocný trh; detail
from the House of
the Black Madonna;
the building itself.*

*Left, detail from Ovocný
trh. Right, the pared down
sign for the Cubist museum.
Far right, the mysterious
caged Madonna.*

❼ Walking east past the theatre brings you to **Ovocný trh**, a large plaza that was once a lively fruit market. At the eastern tip of the plaza stands the **House of the Black Madonna**, named for the figurine encased in a nook on its north-east corner. This is the first Cubist building in Prague, built in 1921 by Josef Gočár, and still an outstanding example of its type. It has become the centre of Cubist history and culture in the city, housing a Cubist museum and gift shop, where you will be amazed to see the number and variety of items that can be rendered in Cubist style. There's also a sweet café upstairs.

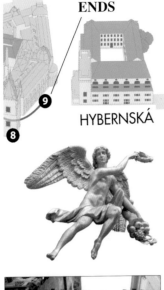

ENDS

HYBERNSKÁ

8 A right turn at the House of the Black Madonna will bring you to the imposing **Powder Tower**, perhaps the most outstanding piece of Gothic architecture in Prague. Started in 1457 as part of the fortifications that once encircled the city, it was originally commissioned to provide security for King Václav IV, who lived practically next door. When he moved to Prague Castle in 1483, the project languished, not really picking up steam again until the late 16th century, when the structure was used to store gunpowder (hence the name). It took a beating in the Prussian siege of 1757, but serious restoration work didn't get underway until 1886, with architect Josef Mocker using the Old Town Bridge Tower (at the eastern end of Charles Bridge) as a model. Today, beneath decades of grime, you can discern statues of kings, saints, angels, animals, gargoyles and elaborate decorative motifs.

Top left, detail from Celetná. Left and above left, the grimy but awe-inspiring Powder Tower. Above, Obecní dům.

9 The Powder Tower is joined to the **Municipal House (Obecní dům)**, an Art Nouveau confection that serves as Prague's primary cultural and social centre. It's one of the most beautiful and significant buildings in the country, built over seven years in the early 1900s on the site of what was once the king's courtyard. All of the country's most famous artists and sculptors were enlisted in the effort, including Alfons Mucha. The results are sumptuous inside and out, crowned by Karel Špilar's tile mosaic *Homage to Prague* atop the central face of the building. The nucleus of the interior is a 2,000-seat concert hall, but there are wonderful decorative touches throughout, including murals, paintings, stained glass and sculptures. There are also several restaurants – pricey, but you're paying for the view and the ambience. If you want to indulge, this is a memorable place to do it.

Historic Heart:
Wenceslas Square

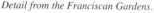

If Old Town Square is the spiritual centre of Prague, this is its historic heart. Wenceslas Square has arguably played host to more momentous events than any single site in the city, particularly in the 20th century. It's where throngs gathered in celebration of the founding of the Czechoslovak Republic in 1918, and in terror when the Nazis marched in and took over in March 1939. The brief burst of hope known as *Detail from the Franciscan Gardens.* the Prague Spring, a period of political liberalization, blossomed here in 1968, but it was another 21 years before the crowds really had something to cheer about, when the Velvet Revolution brought down the Communist government in 1989.

Today Wenceslas Square is the commercial hub of the city, lined with banks, hotels and shops ranging from a Nike superstore to open-air sausage stands. Simply making your way down the square can be difficult in the summer, as cabs dart in and out of sidestreets, crowds of tourists mingle with office workers and police stand at the ready to pull over traffic violators. The middle strip is the best place for sightseeing at the same time as avoiding the hectic crowds. Lively and energetic by day, the square has many pavement cafés offering great vantage points for people watching.

Both the look and character of the square change dramatically after dark, when neon signs light up like electric crowns on top of the buildings and revellers, hustlers and other creatures of the night take over the streets. You can expect to be approached by touts for the strip clubs (they get paid based on how many people they can steer inside), disreputable women

offering their services and drunken tourists asking for directions. It all has a certain garish appeal, and you should be safe if you keep your wits about you, as violent crime is rare in Prague. Keep your valuables safely tucked away (not in a tempting backpack or purse) and don't let anybody put their hands on you: your wallet will vanish as quickly as they do.

The dramatic interior of Our Lady of the Snows.

ENDS

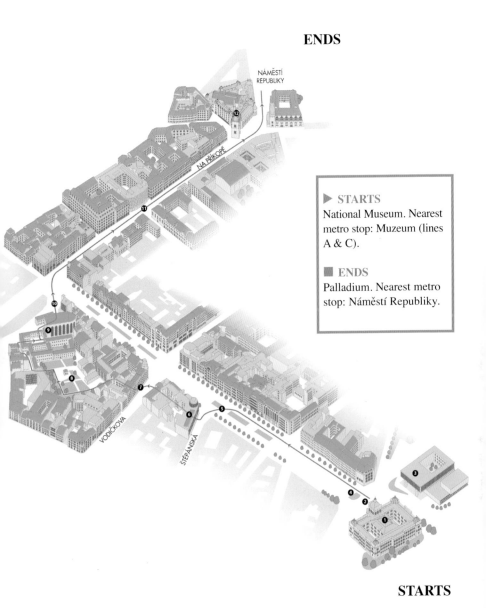

► **STARTS**
National Museum. Nearest metro stop: Muzeum (lines A & C).

■ **ENDS**
Palladium. Nearest metro stop: Náměstí Republiky.

STARTS

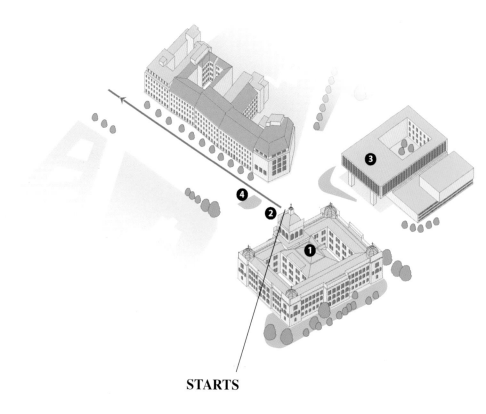

STARTS

❶ **Wenceslas Square** has a decided pitch in elevation, so it's easiest to start at the top - literally - in front of the **National Museum**. Opened in 1818, this huge neo-Renaissance structure boasts an impressive array of statues and other decorative stonework. Long-time residents say it still bears marks of the Russian bullets used to quash the Prague Spring, but for a visitor it would be hard to find any evidence of these beneath a century's worth of grime. Inside, the lobby is breathtaking, with soaring marble columns and twin staircases so large that they double as a concert venue. The exhibits are less interesting, mostly a scattershot collection of fossils and stuffed animal specimens without much information for English speakers.

Nevertheless, the architecture of the museum is worth some time, both inside and out.

The National Museum.

The poignant memorial to Jan Palach.

The former headquarters of Radio Free Europe.

❷ Leave the museum, and walk out on to the cobblestone pavement directly in front, where you will see a jagged bronze cross embedded in the ground, often adorned with flowers or candles keeping vigil. This marks the site where a Czech student named Jan Palach set himself on fire in January 1969 in protest against Soviet oppression. His suicidal act baffled much of the rest of the world, but the Czechs regard him as a political martyr and national hero - as they do Jan Zajíc, who did the same thing a month later. Amid the bustle and bright lights that fill Wenceslas Square today, it's hard to imagine a time, not very long ago, when the lives of Czechoslovaks and the future of their nation seemed so dark that young men were driven to set themselves ablaze to alert the rest of the world.

❸ The **modernist building** immediately west of the National Museum is the former Parliament building where the Federal Assembly met until the Czech and Slovak Republics split in 1993. Afterwards, then-Czech President Václav Havel offered U.S. President Bill Clinton use of the building for a symbolic 1 crown per day if he would relocate Radio Free Europe from its Munich headquarters to Prague, where it has remained since 1995. After the terrorist attacks of September 11, 2001, the building (known among Radio Free Europe

employees as 'the fortress') was surrounded by concrete barricades and ringed with a 24-hour military security. In 2006, Radio Free Europe commissioned a new and more secure building in Prague 10, which it moved into in the summer of 2009, while the former Parliament building is now being renovated as an annexe to the National Museum.

❹ Facing east towards Wenceslas Square, walk across busy **Wilsonova**, and head for 'the horse', the local term for the imposing statue of St Wenceslas astride his mount and the most common meeting point in the city. The original dates back to 1678, though the statue you see today was designed by noted Czech sculptor J.V. Myslbek and put in place in 1912. Subsequently, four statues of Bohemian religious figures were added to the granite base: Sts Agnes, Adalbert, Prokop and Ludmila, Wenceslas's grandmother. The plaque at the base of the stairs commemorates the founding of the first Czechslovak Republic. Continue walking, a few steps down the median, where you will see a headstone with images of Jan Palach and Jan Zajic serving as a memorial to all the victims of Communism.

5 Carry on walking down the Square, picking out any bench to take in the dizzying array of sculptures, murals and *sgraffito* on the surrounding buildings, increasingly lost amid the jumble of shop signs and advertisements. In particular, look out for the splashy murals on the **Wiehl building (no. 36)** and the bizarre set of Assyrian masks on the **Supich building (nos. 38-40)**. The balcony of the **Melantrich building (no. 30)** is where outoing communist President Alexander Dubček and incoming populist President Václav Havel embraced before thousands of people on November 24, 1989, signalling the end of communist rule. You can find out more about Czech history in the English-language section of the excellent **Palác Knih bookstore (no. 41)**, which also has an extensive selection of books on Prague, as well as maps and postcards.

6 Now it's time to explore some of the more interesting byways of Wenceslas Square. Turn on to **Štěpánská**, the third street on your left as you're walking down the square, and look for the domed marquee over the entrance to **Lucerna**, a faded yet still impressive shopping and entertainment complex. In contrast to the glittery Levi's and Marks & Spencer stores on the square, this stately labyrinth houses a charming collection of knick-knack and speciality shops, cafés, the Lucerna

King Wenceslas.

performance hall and music bar (the latter a great venue for rock and jazz shows) and a grand old cinema. Stop at the cinema's elaborate second-floor bar and café (reached via the big marble staircase), which will give you a good perspective on Lucerna's handsome but unpredictable blend of Art Nouveau and Art Deco styles and influences. It's also the best spot to appreciate the hanging statue of St Wenceslas on an upside-down horse, a satirical piece by local art prankster David Černý.

7 Continue through the Lucerna lobby, out the other side on to **Vodičkova**, and cross the street into the **Světozor complex**. Though much smaller than Lucerna, it has a useful selection of lunch spots and a repertory cinema that shows English-language films and Czech films with English subtitles. Světozor also has one of the single most impressive pieces of stained glass in town (outside the churches), a tribute to Nikola Tesla, the famous electrical engineer and inventor who spent the better part of 1880 studying in Prague. Tesla had fond memories of his time here for the rest of his life, and the city regards him as a favourite son. Stop at any electrical supply shop and chances are you will find Tesla appliances or light bulbs on the shelves.

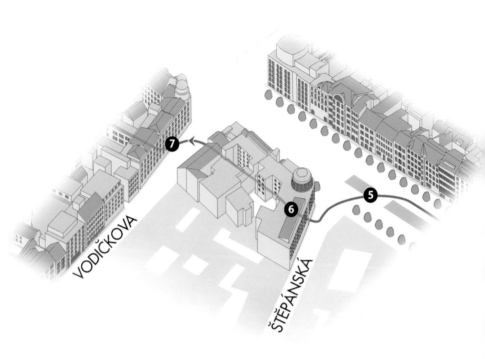

VODIČKOVA

ŠTĚPÁNSKÁ

The Tesla window, left, and the arthouse cinema, right, both in Světozor.

8 As you walk beneath the Tesla window and down the stairs, you will see a gate on your left into the **Franciscan gardens**. The double doors (*right*) are filled with reliefs depicting the life of St Francis of Assisi, but the garden itself has not a whisper of religiosity. In the summer, it's brimming with lush fruit trees, grapevines, colourful flower beds and plenty of benches where you can enjoy a shady break from the hot streets. If the ice cream stand or one of the other take-out counters in Světozor caught your eye, this is the perfect place to stop and enjoy your treat.

Door to the Franciscan gardens.

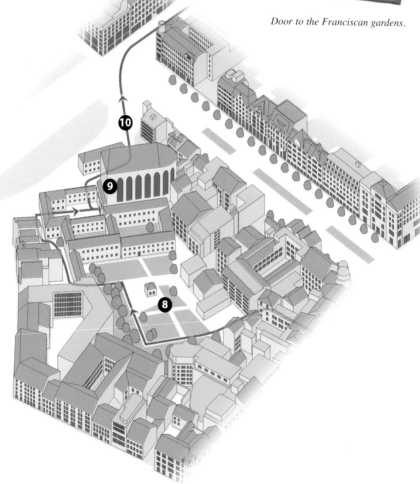

The colourful Franciscan Gardens, above, make an ideal resting place. Right, Our Lady of the Snows.

9 Leave the garden at the corner diagonally opposite the one you entered. The passage will take you to the courtyard entrance (on your right) for **Our Lady of the Snows**, the tallest church building in Prague. The original, commissioned by King Charles IV in 1347, was to have a 40-metre high nave intended to overshadow even St Vitus Cathedral. It didn't quite work out that way, but the resulting 34-metre nave is still dramatic, with a grandiose mural above the main altar that seems to literally reach to heaven. A blend of Gothic and Renaissance architectural styles, Our Lady of the Snows occasionally hosts art exhibitions and concerts.

The glorious interior and towering nave of Our Lady of the Snows.

10 As you leave the church back into the courtyard, go through the doorway on your right and then take a sharp right past the music shop to see one of the city's lesser-known but genuine curiosities: a **Cubist lamp post**. Practically everywhere else in the world, Cubism was strictly a painting style. In Bohemia it was embraced and expanded into architecture and design, with many traces of its influence still visible throughout Prague today. This is one of the most striking examples, worth a whimsical photograph or two.

Cubist lamp post.

49

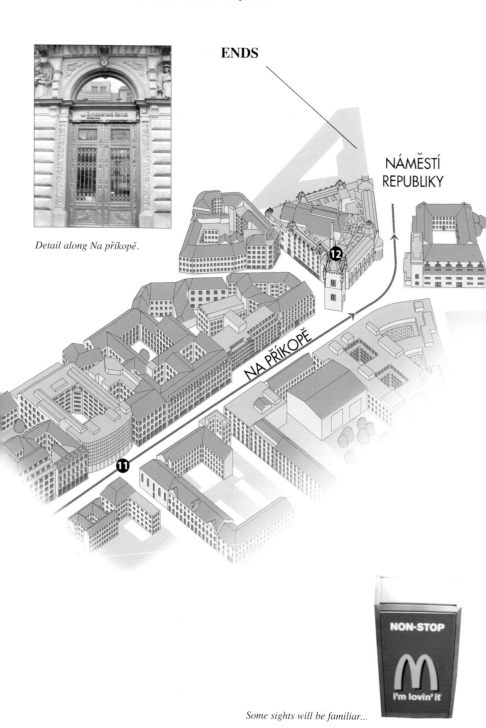

ENDS

NÁMĚSTÍ
REPUBLIKY

Detail along Na příkopě.

NA PŘÍKOPĚ

NON-STOP

i'm lovin' it

Some sights will be familiar...

⓫ Continuing around the corner past **Bata**, the famous shoe store, and **Dům Knihy**, *right*, a bookstore with few English language books but a lovely second-floor café, will bring you to the bottom of Wenceslas Square and the corner of **Na příkopě**, Prague's main high street. In keeping with its counterparts throughout the world, this one has everything from Swedish retailer H&M to American chain restaurant TGI Friday's. It's interesting not so much for what's here now as for what used to be – a moat (Na příkopě means 'on the moat'),

ages ago, and more recently, dreary communist shops and government offices. You can get a taste by stopping in the expensive but fascinating **Museum of Communism (no. 10**, above the McDonald's). It's a pleasant stroll down Na příkopě, but watch your belongings: the stylish shops and wealthy clientele also attract a steady stream of pickpockets.

⓬ Continue along Na příkopě until you reach (north-eastwards) **Obecní dům** (see Old Town Walk). Turn left on to **náměstí Republiky**, which offers one of the city's most dramatic contrasts in pre- and post-revolution economics: the new **Palladium shopping mall** and, directly across the street, the ancient **Kotva department store**. The latter is a relic of socialism, with a second-rate selection of seemingly everything one needs in life, from clothing to car parts, crammed into a single building. The Palladium is a 7.5 billion-crown (£260m) refurbishment project that turned a massive disused army barracks building into 19,500 square

Side view of the glitzy new Palladium shopping complex.

metres of glittery business, retail and entertainment space. It would be big but unremarkable in most Western European cities. Here, it offers a dramatic example of how far Prague has come in the relatively short time since freedom was declared on Wenceslas Square.

The front of the new Divadlo Hybernia theatre, formerly a Baroque monastery.

Chopin watches the crowds in náměstí Republiky.

Prague Castle: from the front gates to Malostranská

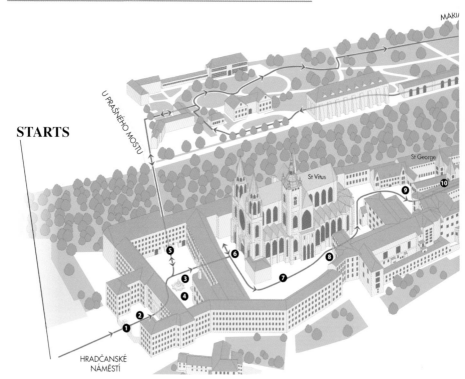

STARTS

U PRAŠNÉHO MOSTU

MARI/

St George

St Vitus

HRADČANSKÉ NÁMĚSTÍ

Floating on the Prague skyline like a fairy tale, Prague Castle occupies the geographic and symbolic high point of the city. It has been a seat of government for 12 centuries, a fortress, a centre of European science and culture, and a commanding throne for rulers ranging from Charles IV to Adolf Hitler. The continuing battle over who owns and should operate St Vitus Cathedral – church or state – reflects the Castle's dual secular and spiritual heritage, which are inextricably intertwined. For the Czech nation, the Castle remains the centre of political gravity and pre-eminent symbol of the country's history and pride.

Less an actual castle than a walled complex of disparate buildings, Prague Castle grew in pieces over hundreds of years, starting with a fortification built in the latter half of the 9th century on what is a natural strategic overlook. The early growth was mostly religious – a bishopric was established on the site in 972 – and it wasn't until 1135 that Prince Soběslav started building a royal palace with walled fortifications. The foundation

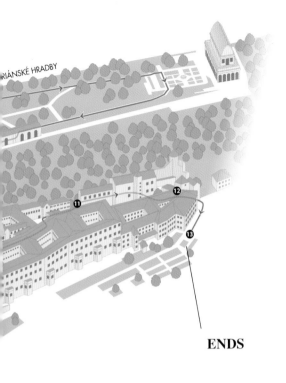

RIÁNSKÉ HRADBY

⑪ ⑫ ⑬

ENDS

*One of the array of
stained glass windows
inside St Vitus Cathedral.*

stone for what is now St Vitus was laid in 1344, with final construction of the stunning Neo-Gothic façade completed in 1929. Extensive renovation of the entire castle complex began during the National Revival of the late 1800s and extended well into the 20th century, restoring many of the interiors and giving the courtyards and gardens a fresh, modern look.

Everyone who comes to Prague visits Prague Castle, which means you're unlikely to find an uncrowded moment there. To avoid the crush, it helps to arrive early in the morning or late in the afternoon. You may also want to consider skipping some of the more popular tourist attractions and spending time in the less-visited gardens and buildings on the north and south grounds adjacent to the Castle. Or come at night, when the lighting is dramatic and the complex nearly deserted. You won't be able to see any of the halls or churches that are open during the day, but the quiet moments to absorb and marvel at centuries of living history are well worth it.

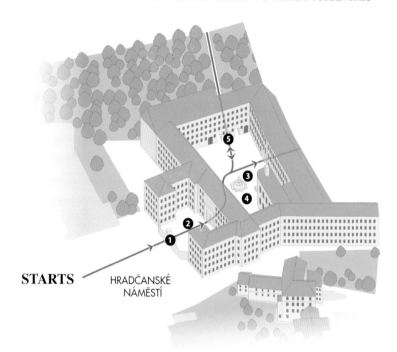

STARTS — HRADČANSKÉ NÁMĚSTÍ

Detail from the main gates of the Castle: the lion represents the Czech kingdom.

❶ The main gate of **Prague Castle**, facing **Hradčanské náměstí**, features a dual set of guards: uniformed human guards stationed in twin zebra-striped alcoves, and towering above them, imposing statues of giants clubbing their enemies to death. The giants are replicas of sculptures originally created by Ignác František Platzer in the 1770s. Topping the flanking pillars are statues symbolizing the Czech kingdom (a lion) and the Habsburg

monarchy (an eagle). The guards wear uniforms designed by Theodor Pištěk, the costume designer for Miloš Forman's films Valmont and Amadeus, who was hired by former Czech President Václav Havel as part of his efforts to brighten and modernize the Castle during his tenure in the 1990s.

Standing guard.

❷ Havel also initiated the elaborate changing of the guard ceremony that takes place at noon every day in the first courtyard, just inside the front gate. The dominant feature of the courtyard is the **Matthias Gate**, a Baroque creation of the early 1600s modelled on the Roman triumphal arches. It is named for the Emperor Matthias, whose titles are listed on the gold plaque above the imperial insignia, with symbols of the countries he ruled in a row beneath. The guards change hourly, but the noon ceremony, with its lively horn fanfare, is the one to catch. Be sure to position yourself to the left (north) side of the gate for the best viewing. Otherwise, when the guards set out the ropes to maintain access through the gate, you will be shunted to the right, where you won't be able to see through the crowd.

The impressive Matthias gate, where you can watch the changing of the guard.

❸ Passing through the Matthias gate brings you to the second courtyard, where the centrepiece is a **Baroque fountain**. This serves as a reminder of Prague Castle's medieval heritage, when the castle needed its own food and water supply while it was under siege. The castle wells were thought to be protected by a dedicated water sprite, Pakit, notable for living underground rather than in a stream or river. The façades of the surrounding buildings, like those in the first courtyard, were created by Viennese architect Nicolo Picassi, who oversaw the rebuilding of the Castle complex after the Prussian siege and occupation of the mid-1700s. Newer touches throughout the Castle, like the twin tapering flagpoles that frame the Matthias Gate in the first courtyard, are the work of famous Slovenian architect Josip Plečnik, hired in the 1920s by Czechoslovak President Tomáš Garrigue Masaryk to renovate the Castle grounds.

Exhibitions at the Castle's galleries. Late 16th/ early 17thC King Rudolf II was an enthusiastic arts patron. Some of his collection is on show here.

❹ You need not buy a ticket, available at the ticket office in the second courtyard, to walk through most of the Castle grounds, which are free and open to the public. However, to get inside most of the churches and historic buildings, and walk along Golden Lane, you will need the cheaper of the two tickets (250 Kč as this guide went to press). The more expensive ticket (350 Kč) will also give you access to the art galleries. Which you choose depends on your interests and tastes, and how much time you want to devote to the Castle, where you could easily spend the better part of a day. On the premise that you've come too far to be deterred by a small admission fee, this walk continues using the cheaper ticket, the best value for money.

5 If you are inclined to wander, the passage way on the left (north) side of the second courtyard leads to **Prašný bridge** and entrances to the **northern Royal Gardens**, which have a splendid series of fountains and regal summer houses that have been converted to art galleries. (You can also tour the gardens as a separate walk by taking tram 22 from the city centre to the Pražský hrad stop.) Our walk through the castle complex continues by taking the passage way east out of the second courtyard, which brings you to the third courtyard and face-to-face, literally, with **St Vitus Cathedral**.

6 One of the largest Gothic cathedrals in Europe, St Vitus can be divided roughly into two parts: the original Gothic eastern half (the rear if you're facing the front), and the Neo-Gothic western half, with its astoundingly rich, detailed façade and 97 m-high lookout tower. It is

The stunning façade of St Vitus.

impossible to overstate the symbolic importance of this breathtaking structure, which serves as the burial place of Czech kings and saints, the repository for the crown jewels (which takes seven separate keys to unlock) and a monumental gallery of wall murals and stained-glass windows – including one by Alfons Mucha – that recount virtually every significant moment in Czech political and religious

history. It's an inspirational place in every sense of the word, and most of it you can see for free: the photos on this page hardly do justice to it. The tombs and rear nave require a ticket.

Above left and right, detail from the exterior of St Vitus.

Mucha's glorious window.

7 Continuing through the third courtyard, you will pass an obelisk designed by Josip Plečnik as a memorial to the First World War dead, a statue of St George slaying the dragon, and a remarkable tile mosaic of The Last Judgment on the south face of the cathedral, a restored work of quartz and glass originally composed in 1370. Further along, after you pass under the archway connecting the cathedral to the **Old Royal Palace**, a large tombstone honours St John Nepomuk (who is buried inside the cathedral), cradled in the arms of an angel. The third courtyard is also the best place to see the impressive array of gargoyles perched along the cathedral roofline. In medieval times, they served not only to siphon water away from the building, but to scare away demons, who were said to be frightened by their own image.

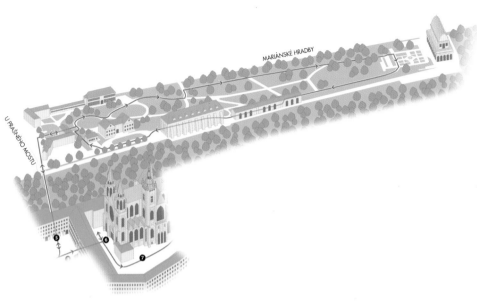

Tombstone of St John Nepomuk.

St George slays the dragon.

Above left, the obelisk memorial. Above centre and right, elaborate grillwork on the side of St Vitus.

8 On the east side of the courtyard opposite the cathedral, the Old Royal Palace was the original residence of Czech kings. Expanded and renovated many times since it was first built in 1135, it has several features of interest. Spacious **Vladislav Hall**, where the National Assembly meets to elect the Czech president, combines two architectural periods with its vaulted Gothic ceiling and squared Romanesque windows. The very wide **Riders Staircase**, reached through a door in the centre of the north wall, was built that way to accommodate knights entering on horseback (during the era the hall was reputedly used for jousting tournaments). A small door to the right of the chapel on the east wall provides egress to a small balcony that offers a marvellous view of the city.

The fountain in St George's Square.

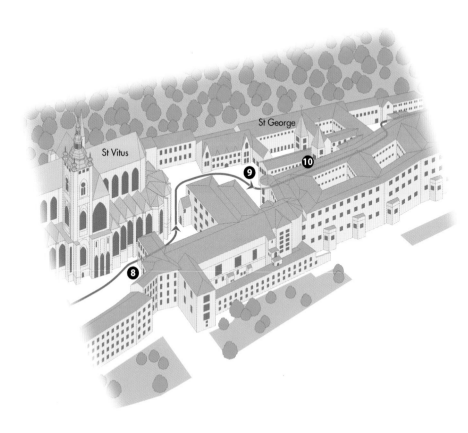

⑨ Leaving the Old Royal Palace via the Riders Staircase drops you into **Jiřské náměstí** (St George's Square), steps away from the twin-steepled **St George's Basilica**. According to one legend, the fatter tower on the right represents Adam, watching protectively over the slender tower on the left, Eve. The basilica's Baroque façade masks the oldest building currently standing in the Prague Castle complex, which is more evident when you step inside and see the

St George's Basilica.

long, dark Romanesque interior. Inside, you will also find chapels dedicated to two Bohemian favourites: St Ludmila, which includes her tomb, and St John Nepomuk, an 18th century addition which is not always open for viewing.

⑩ Continuing past St George's along what is marked as **Jiřská street**, you will pass a very long building on the right known as the **Home for Noblewomen**. Established in 1755 by Empress Maria Theresa for impoverished female aristocrats, it now houses administrative

Carved detail from the Basilica.

offices for the Castle. Before you get to the next building on the right, **Lobkowicz Palace**, which is filled with the heirlooms of a once-exiled noble Bohemian family, you will see a small street to your left that leads to **Golden Lane**.

The new Burgrave's Bureau.

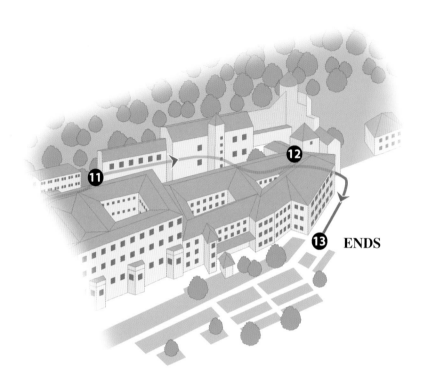

ENDS

🔴 Though this is one of the most famous streets in Prague, in the 19th century Golden Lane, named for the goldsmiths who once lived there, was inhabited mostly by artisans and the poor. Now filled with souvenir shops, the street is anchored at each end by a tower. On the west end, where you enter, the **White Tower** was a prison for nobility and the clergy. **Dalibor Tower**, at the other end of the street, was the most notorious dungeon in the Castle, and is still a very creepy place. Almost every house on the street comes with a legend or interesting bit of history. The blue house at **no. 22** is where

Golden Lane and Kafka's blue house.

Franz Kafka lived and wrote in 1920. The house at **no. 14** was occupied by a fortune teller named Madame de Thebes, who was killed by Nazis during the Second World War after she foretold their defeat. Organ music is said to emanate from the house at **no. 20** at midnight on Good Friday every year. And the most intriguing house on the street may be hidden from human eyes. The Golem author Gustav Meyrink wrote of an invisible dwelling, the House at the Last Lantern, which serves as a gateway between the visible and invisible worlds.

Statue in the Burgrave's courtyard.

⑫ From Dalibor Tower, a walkway along the ramparts leads to the passage way to the **Burgrave's residence and courtyard**, a pleasant place to stop for coffee and do some souvenir shopping. In the summer, Shakespeare plays are staged in the courtyard – a great setting, though the performances are not very accommodating to tourists, as they are all in Czech. Leave the courtyard through the main entrance, where a left turn takes you past the **Black Tower** to the eastern entrance gate of the castle. A few steps down the entrance

Dalibor Tower.

ramp, there is a viewpoint with telescopes: the view is particularly impressive at night. From here you can continue down the steps, which will drop you near the Malostranská tram and subway stop. If it's summer, turn instead back and to the right, where a small entry leads to the lovely **southern gardens**.

⑬ There is no sweeter place in Prague to spend a summer afternoon than this set of formal terraced gardens, which offer a number of outstanding

The stunning view from the observation point.

lookout points and one of the most bewildering collections of outdoor sculptures in the city: a Baroque fountain, a limestone pyramid, obelisks, a giant bowl (designed as a female counterpoint to the obelisks) and pavilions in a variety of styles. The wing of the Old Royal Palace that juts out into the garden was the site of another famous defenestration. Twin sandstone obelisks mark the spot where two governors were thrown out the window of what was the Czech Chancellery in 1618. They survived – according to legend, because the Virgin Mary caught them in her cloak. The more prosaic and likely explanation is the one offered by a chronicler of the period: The spot was a popular rubbish heap, and they landed in a pile 'ruffled as a heap of dung and soft'. After your soft landing in this verdant setting, you can either continue to the western garden entrance, which brings you back to our starting point, Hradčanské náměstí, or retrace your steps to the eastern entrance gate. Descend the long stone staircase to Klárov street and turn right. Walk past the Malostranská metro stop and across the Mánes bridge and you will be at the Rudolfinum, the starting point for the 'Josefov' walk (page 18).

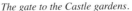
The gate to the Castle gardens.

Power and the glory: Hradčany

Everyone who visits Prague makes the pilgrimage to Prague Castle, but the neighbourhood behind the castle, known as Hradčany, is in many ways equally interesting. Founded as a separate borough in 1320, it grew in pieces to include Pohořelec, Strahov and Petřín, all of which formally became part of Prague in 1784. The area in front of the castle gates, which burned down in 1541, was rebuilt in grand fashion over subsequent decades by noblemen who wanted residences close to the seat of Habsburg power. Today Hradčany is a serene mix of monumental palaces and towering churches, interspersed with souvenir shops, restaurants and cafés, set on

STARTS

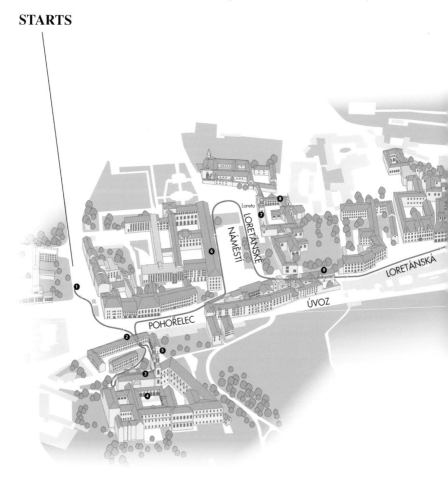

broad cobbled streets and squares. While the castle is always a bustle of activity, and below, Malá Strana teems with tourists and government workers, Hradčany is a world apart, quiet and deep with historic intrigue.

This walk follows the main artery of Hradčany, stopping at the most interesting sights along the way, but as you walk you will see winding passages, narrow stairways and walled streets veering off to the left and right. By all means, explore these if the spirit moves you. They may lead to nothing more than a locked gate, or they may open on to a magical hidden courtyard or an unexpected view of the city. Either way, you'll find that Hradčany has many small secrets and charms for the inquisitive visitor.

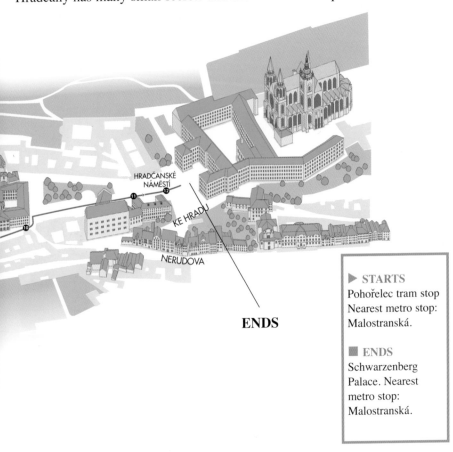

HRADČANSKÉ NÁMĚSTÍ

KE HRADU

NERUDOVA

ENDS

▶ **STARTS**
Pohořelec tram stop
Nearest metro stop:
Malostranská.

■ **ENDS**
Schwarzenberg
Palace. Nearest
metro stop:
Malostranská.

STARTS

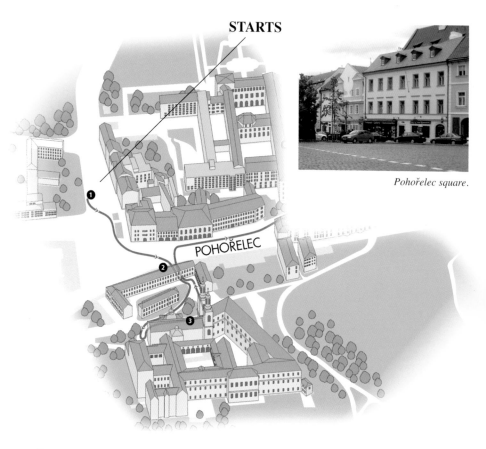

Pohořelec square.

POHOŘELEC

❶ A convenient starting point is the **Pohořelec tram stop**, watched over by the imposing statues of astronomers Johannes Kepler (on the left) and Tycho Brahe. The two men worked together, not always happily, in the court of Emperor Rudolf II in the early 1600s. Brahe, a Dane invited to serve as Rudolf's official court astronomer and astrologer, had the best observations of the heavens at the time, but needed Kepler, a German mathematician, to make sense of them. Kepler didn't get full access to the data until after Brahe died in October 1601, under mysterious circumstances that have given rise to centuries of conspiracy theories, including speculation that Kepler had a hand in Brahe's demise. What's certain is that Kepler used the data to formulate the laws of planetary motion, affirming the Copernican theory of the universe (in which the planets revolve around the sun) and revolutionizing astronomy.

The imposing statue.

Above left, entrance to Strahov Monastery. Above right, the peaceful courtyard.

❷ Your first stop is **Strahov Monastery**, which is a little tricky to reach. Cross **Keplerova street** towards the **Slava Gallery**, turn right and cross **Pohořelec street**, then turn left and start walking towards the Castle. In between **nos 7 and 9** you will see an entry to an ascending stairway marked by an insignia of a bishop flanked by a snake and olive tree - the bishop being St Norbert, the founder of the Premonstratensian Order, which established the monastery in 1140. Go up the stairs and when you come out, follow the low wall to your right through the courtyard to the monastery entrance.

❸ Before entering the monastery, stop for a look inside the adjacent **Church of the Assumption of Our Lady**, with its rich trove of artwork. First built in the 12th century in Romanesque style, and rebuilt many times since, the church is elaborately decorated with wall murals and ceiling frescoes – 46 of the latter in the main nave, portraying a colourful variety of Biblical scenes ranging from that of Moses and the burning bush to Samson with a dead lion. The Virgin Mary stands watch above the front door, from the main altar and in many of the frescoes in between, which were painted in the mid-1700s. During a visit to Prague in 1787, Mozart played the organ in this church.

Left to right: the elaborate façade, doorway and interior of the Church of the Assumption of Our Lady.

Left to right: the huge, golden Philosophical Hall; the heavily decorated Theological Hall; a treasure from the monastery's varied collection.

4 Leave the church and enter the main attraction, Strahov Monastery. It's a large complex, only a small portion of which is open to the public, but what you can see is truly remarkable. There are two **libraries** open for viewing, though unfortunately only from the doorways, as they're too fragile to withstand a constant parade of tourists. The massive, musty **Philosophical Hall** holds 50,000 volumes of scientific literature and boasts an elaborate ceiling fresco that traces the spiritual development of mankind. The smaller **Theological Hall** contains 18,000 books and a sumptuous set of statues along with the frescoes in the stuccoed ceiling. Be sure to explore the cabinets in the hallway that connects the two halls, which are filled with fascinating donations made by visitors to the monastery over the centuries, mostly preserved specimens of exotic animals such as an octopus, a giant crab and a dodo bird.

5 Upon leaving the monastery, there are two pleasant places to stop for refreshment before you retrace your steps to Pohořelec. Directly across the courtyard, **Klasterni Pivovar Strahov** is a restaurant that makes its own beer. Try the *Svatá Norbert*, a good dark lager. Alternatively, go through the archway on your right before you get to the stairway, where you'll find a picturesque view of the city from the **Bellavista** restaurant, perched above the monastery orchard. If the Bellavista is too pricey, or closed for the season, simply walk past the restaurant and look for the benches along the path to your right, where you can enjoy the same view for free.

6 Having retraced your steps, continue along Pohořelec, which quickly splits. Follow the left fork, **Loretánská street**. A short walk will bring you to **Loretánské náměstí**, a square flanked by two large buildings. The enormous, 150-metre long building on the west side is **Černín Palace**, once the home of the emperor's ambassador to Venice and now the Czech Ministry of Foreign Affairs. Though it looks calm, the building is notorious in 20thC history. The Gestapo used it for interrogations during the Nazi occupation, and in 1948, Czechoslovak Foreign Minister Jan Masaryk was found dead on the sidewalk in front of the building. Officially, he was said to have either fallen or jumped from an upstairs window. But Masaryk was one of the last opponents of the looming communist takeover, and was more likely a victim of defenestration – that is, literally throwing someone out the window, a favoured method of political assassination in the Czech lands.

Colourful billboards along Pohořelec.

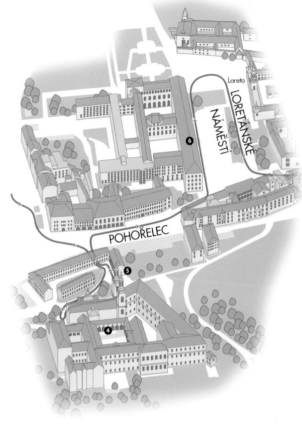

Edvard Beneš, second president of Czechoslovakia.

View from the Bellavista restaurant.

The Černín Palace has a dramatic history.

The front of the Loreto.

❼ Across the square, the magnificent **Loreto** is the single most amazing religious structure in Prague. A shrine built after the Thirty Years' War (1618-1648) to foster Catholicism, the Loreto is a baroque fantasy of sculptured angels, saints and Biblical scenes, eye-popping religious treasures and a particularly macabre style of veneration. The exterior walls were built in the 1660s to enclose the original structure, the **Santa Casa Chapel**, which is still the centrepiece of the Loreto complex. It is said to be a replica of the building in Nazareth in which the Virgin Mary was visited by the Archangel Gabriel to announce she would be the mother of Christ. The Santa Casa feels more creepy than inspirational, with a mysterious black Madonna almost hidden in a well-protected silver sanctuary.

One of two Baroque fountains in the Loreto courtyard.

Counter-clockwise from top left: exterior of Santa Casa, interior of Santa Casa, two interiors from the Church of the Nativity.

❽ Don't leave the Loreto without taking in at least two other sights. **The Church of the Nativity**, adjacent to the Santa Casa chapel, offers an homage to lesser-known martyrs in gruesome detail. The angels on the front left side altar are holding a pair of pliers and a tooth, honouring St Apollonia, who was tortured by having her teeth torn out; the angels to the right of the opposite altar are holding a platter with a pair of breasts to honor poor St Agatha, who had hers cut off. The reliquaries on either side of the main altar contain the real deal - actual mummified bodies of saints (St Felicissimo on the left, St Marcia on the right) dressed in period clothing. If that all gets to be too much, make your way to the second floor of the main building, where you'll find a 'treasury room' of priceless religious artefacts, including a monstrance encrusted with more than 6,000 tiny diamonds.

Above left, the atmospheric Black Ox pub. Above right, grand gate along Loretánská.

Children will love the toy shop on Loretánská.

❾ After that dip into the sacred and profane, you'll probably need a drink, so retrace your steps back on to Loretánská, walking towards the Castle, stopping at U âerného Vola (The Black Ox, no. 1) where you can also enjoy a cultural curiosity. This is the last pub of its kind in Hradãany, a smoky, noisy Czech beer hall with old wooden tables and benches and the cheapest beer in the area. While everything else in this neighbourhood went upmarket after the Velvet Revolution, this pub stubbornly stuck to its roots, and remains a throwback amid the stylish cafés and restaurants that have grown up around it. If service is slow and surly, the benches crowded and the smoke so thick you can cut it with a knife, you're in the right place.

10 As you continue down Loretánská, you will see an elaborate street lamp. This is reputedly the first gas lamp ever in Prague. Further along, the street opens into a **large square** with a **small park** that has a sculpted column at the far end. This is a plague column, built in the early 1700s by survivors of the Black Plague in thanksgiving for still being alive. If you travel throughout the Czech Republic, you will find many of these on town squares. This one is built in a Baroque style with, as is customary, the Virgin Mary on the top and local saints around the base.

Far left, the first gas lamp. Left, the plague column.

Hradčanské náměstí.

11 A few more steps will bring you to the middle of **Hradčanské náměstí**, where you can see all the ornate palaces that were built after the great fire of 1541. At the west end of the square, facing the park, is the early Baroque **Tuscan Palace (Toskánský palác, no. 5)**, now an annexe for the Ministry of Foreign Affairs. To the north side of the square, from left to right as you're facing the buildings, is the **Martinic Palace (no. 8)**, a Renaissance building with decorative motifs now used for city government offices. **Sternberg Palace (no. 15)**, built in the early 1700s and beautifully restored in recent years, houses the National Gallery's collection of European Old Masters. And the 16thC **Archbishop's Palace (no. 16)**, has a fancy Rococo façade. Looking across to the south side of the square, the imposing **Schwarzenberg Palace (no. 2)**, with its elaborate sgraffito decoration, is regarded as the finest Renaissance building in the city. It is now a military museum.

LORETÁNSKÁ

12 The walk ends next to **Schwarzenberg Palace**, at the **statue of Tomáš Garrigue Masaryk**, one of the most revered Czech political figures of the 20th century. Masaryk was the key figure in forging an independent Czechoslovak state between the world wars, and served as the country's first president from 1920 to 1935. (It was his son Jan who was found dead at Černín Palace, see **6**.) From here you can

Left, statue of Masaryk. Above, ornate gateway into the palace.

continue on to the start of the walk through Malá Strana (page 90), or jump ahead to the 'Prague Castle' walk that begins at the Palace gates (page 52). This walk ends here, with close access to the no.22 tram line.

Top left and left, the Schwarzenberg Palace.

Detail from Hradčanské náměstí.

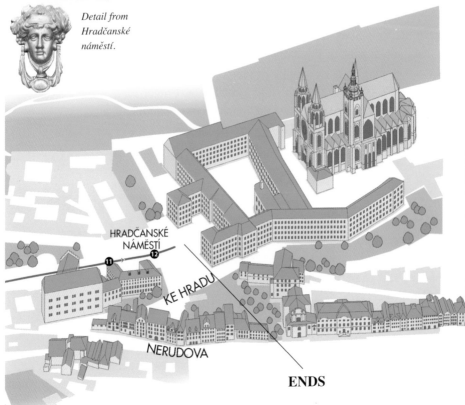

HRADČANSKÉ NÁMĚSTÍ

11 ➤ **12**

KE HRADU

NERUDOVA

ENDS

71

Green Retreat: Petřín Hill

At some point you will want to escape the narrow, often crowded streets of the city and enjoy a refreshing stroll through greenery and open spaces. There is no better place for this than Petřín (pronounced *Pet-cheen*) hill, a verdant retreat easily accessible from many points in Malá Strana and an endlessly fascinating place to explore.

Essentially one large park that reaches from Strahov Monastery on the north end to Prague's Smíchov neighbourhood on the south, Petřín offers an extensive network of shaded walkways, benches and other perches with great views of the city, monuments and tourist attractions. A large part of the eastern face of the hill once comprised the royal orchards, and is still covered with apple, pear and cherry trees. Fallen fruit covers the hillside in the autumn, though as the trees have not been tended in a long time, most of it is bitter. And this being the Czech Republic, even when you seem to be well in the woods, you're never far from a cold beer. Linger for a while if you can at an attractive spot or one of the many grassy redoubts just off the pathways. In the noise and bustle of the city, it's easy to miss Prague's

An extravagantly dressed lady ushers visitors into the Vrtba Gardens.

magical side. Here, as the light changes and breezes whisper through the trees, legends and spirits will come to life if you are calm and receptive.

The sweeping views from Petřín Hill and the Nebozízek funicular stop - see ❷.

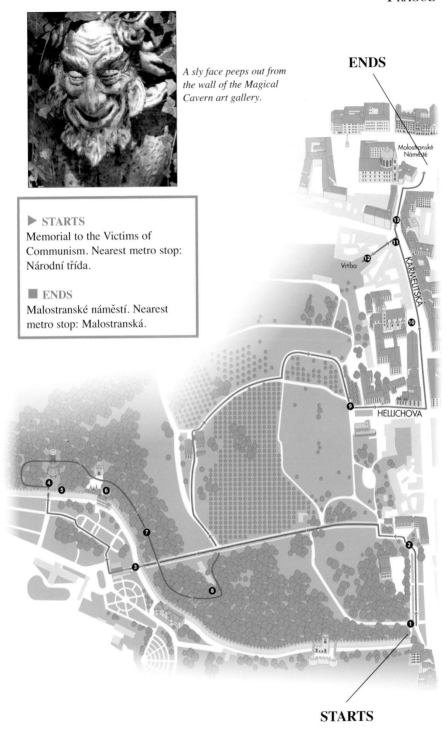

A sly face peeps out from the wall of the Magical Cavern art gallery.

ENDS

▶ **STARTS**
Memorial to the Victims of Communism. Nearest metro stop: Národní třída.

■ **ENDS**
Malostranské náměstí. Nearest metro stop: Malostranská.

STARTS

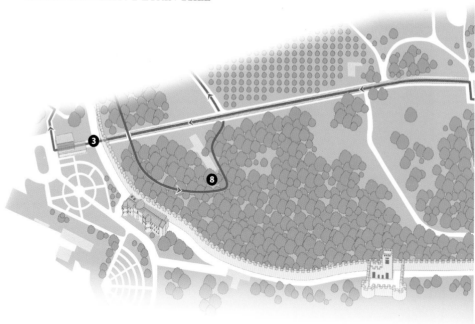

The poignant, unsettling Memorial to the Victims of Communism, at the start of the walk.

1 Though this is a light-hearted walk, we start on a somber note, at the **Memorial to the Victims of Communism** located just up the embankment from the **Ujezd tram stop**. The receding series of disintegrating figures by Czech sculptor Olbram Zoubek offers a powerful and eloquent testimony to the corrosive effects of tyranny on the human spirit. The metal ribbon that runs up the middle of the steps leading to the sculpture tallies the impact of communist rule in the Czech Republic in more prosaic but no less devastating terms (though unfortunately in Czech): 205,486 arrested, 284 beheaded or hanged, 327 shot crossing the border, and so on.

2 A short walk north (to your right) from the monument brings you to the entrance for the **funicular**, which you can ride with a standard tram ticket. The 510-m line began running in 1891, originally on water power. It was shut down in 1914, reopening in 1932 powered by electricity. An estimated 1.3 million people ride the funicular annually, so if you go on a sunny summer day, expect a line. You can walk up the hillside if you don't want to wait, but it's more fun to ride these antique cars and watch the city come into view as you ascend the hillside. There is one stop on the way to the top, at a pricey restaurant: resist the temptation and stay on board.

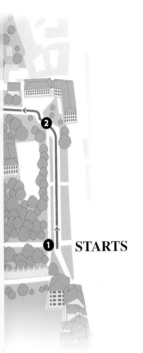

3 When you leave the station house at the top, on your left you will see a large rose garden, which is worth a stroll on a sunny day. You will also see the distinctive dome of **Štefánik Observatory**, where there are telescopes for viewing – if the sky is clear, sunspots by day and the moon, planets and deep sky at night. There are some good exhibits inside, though not all in English, as well as occasional English-language guided

STARTS tours. (Check www.observatory.cz for a complete schedule.)

Milan Rastislav Štefánik: astronomer, politician, art connoisseur and general.

Watch the sky from the Štefánik Observatory, above, then wander through the beautiful rose gardens, below.

Give your feet a rest and let the electric-powered funicular railway do the work.

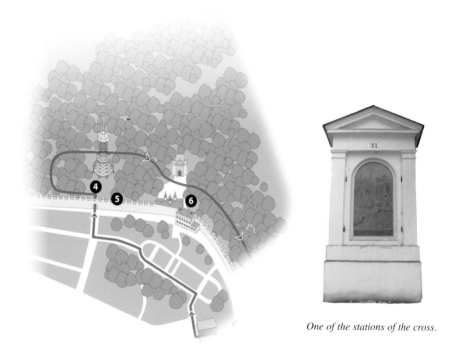

One of the stations of the cross.

❹ Going to your right from the station house takes you down a ramp into another rose garden. Follow the ashphalt walkway out the other side, turn right at the first crossing path and go through the archway, which will bring you to the base of **Petřín Tower**. This charming one-fifth-scale copy of the Eiffel Tower was built in 1891 for the city's Jubilee Exhibiton. It's the most dominant feature on the city skyline at night, and by day offers arguably the best view of Prague. However, it calls for a little effort: you climb 299 steps that wrap around the outside of the tower, and it can be a dizzying ascent if you don't have a head for heights. Don't think about it, make the climb and enjoy the view, which is spectacular.

Petřín Tower.

❺ Of the many features you can see from the top that aren't readily apparent on the ground, the most arresting is the **Hunger Wall**, a monolith that winds its way from the base of Petřín Hill up and across the top (you passed under it when you went through the arch). Though the wall had practical defensive purposes, it was basically a make-work project initiated by King Charles IV in 1360 to help his starving subjects feed themselves. If you get a chance when you're back on the ground, take a closer look at the wall. Even rebuilt many times over the centuries, it's an astounding edifice, 8 m high and 2 m thick in places, with an occasional battlement still in place.

❻ The area around the base of the tower is filled with curiosities. The fairy-tale castle, also built in 1891 for the Jubilee, houses the **Mirror Maze**, a fun-house attraction of skewed mirrors for the kids. The Baroque **Church of St Lawrence** is unfortunately open only for services. But you can have a religious experience of sorts by following the large stone stations of the cross that dot the hill top. Or relax over coffee or a beer in the café at the base of the tower, which also offers outside tables that are great for people watching.

The fantastical Mirror Maze.

The enormous Hunger Wall.

7 There are many paths down from the top. If you take the one between the Mirror Maze and St. Lawrence church, it will take you on a pleasant walk that winds down the eastern face of the hill, with plenty of spots to veer off the path for great views. About halfway down, you will come to a small structure that is impossible to miss, festooned with fairies and demons. Even for Petřín, this is an oddity: an art gallery called the **Magical Cavern**, decorated like a wizard's hideaway and filled with fantastical paintings by one man, a bearded fellow who calls himself Reon. The gallery is open only sporadically, but if he's there and you're interested, he will give you a personal tour in English.

Inside the Magican Cavern.

8 Shortly beyond the Magical Cavern, the path opens on to the expansive patio of **Nebozízek**, a small but well-appointed hotel and restaurant. Food is expensive here, but this is a lovely place to stop for ice cream or a drink, with a fabulous view of the city. Or sit on one of the benches under the tree, where you don't have to buy anything and can enjoy the same view. Alternatively, continue down the path (which goes under the funicular) to **Petřínské Terasy**, a larger and less expensive restaurant with excellent views. This is a popular place for weddings and other celebrations, so be forewarned that on weekends in the summer, it may not be open to the public.

7

Relaxing and admiring the view in Nebozízek, with its ornate fountain (right).

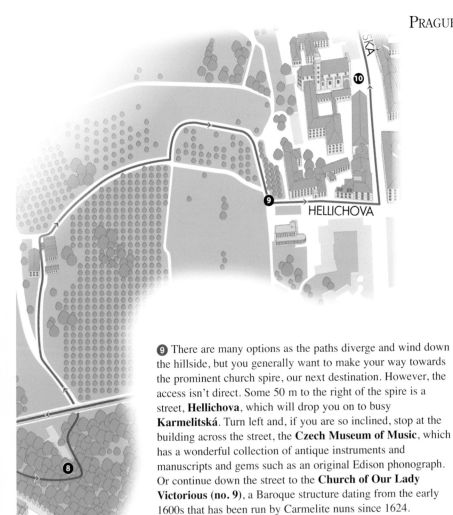

HELLICHOVA

9 There are many options as the paths diverge and wind down the hillside, but you generally want to make your way towards the prominent church spire, our next destination. However, the access isn't direct. Some 50 m to the right of the spire is a street, **Hellichova**, which will drop you on to busy **Karmelitská**. Turn left and, if you are so inclined, stop at the building across the street, the **Czech Museum of Music**, which has a wonderful collection of antique instruments and manuscripts and gems such as an original Edison phonograph. Or continue down the street to the **Church of Our Lady Victorious (no. 9)**, a Baroque structure dating from the early 1600s that has been run by Carmelite nuns since 1624.

10 Inside the church is a truly world-class religious icon: *Il Bambino de Praga*, the Infant of Prague, a wax effigy of the Christ child brought from Spain to Prague in 1628. Roman Catholics around the world pray to the Infant, and the mosaic of thanksgiving plaques surrounding the splendiferous gold and marble altar where the statue is displayed are only one indication of how many miracles have been attributed to him. The prayer cards in 13 languages suggest how far pilgrims come to offer their prayers in person. Though the church is a sacred Catholic shrine, it also has a secular side. Upstairs, a museum displays the Infant's many fabulous outfits, hand-crafted by devoted believers. And don't miss the souvenir shop in the back, where you can take home the Infant embroidered on t-shirts – if you like.

The Church of Our Lady Victorious.

⓫ Back on Karmelitská, turn left and walk past the many souvenir shop windows displaying Infant of Prague figurines to a plain doorway (on the same side of the street as the church) marked **Vrtbovská Zahrada**. This unremarkable entrance takes you to Vrtba Garden, the loveliest Baroque terraced garden in Prague. First laid out in 1720, the garden is noteworthy for its imaginative layout, skilful blend of colours and extensive statuary. As you ascend the terraces, each has something special to offer.

Images, motifs and figurines of The Infant of Prague are everywhere.

⓬ Access to the garden is through a *sala terrena* decorated with murals celebrating the arts and sciences, flanked by statues of Ceres and Bacchus. In the fountain on the first level outside, a cherub wrestles with a dragon. On the second level, the symmetrical gardens are framed by sculpted hedges and ascending ballustrades decorated with vases. The third level offers an array of Roman gods: Vulcan, Apollo, Diana, Juno, Minerva, Jupiter and Mars. That terrace slopes up to a gloriette decorated with mermaids, sea shells and other elements that invoke the life aquatic. The doorway on the right of the gloriette will take you to the very top, which offers a fabulous view of Prague Castle, St Nicholas church and other landmarks of Malá Strana.

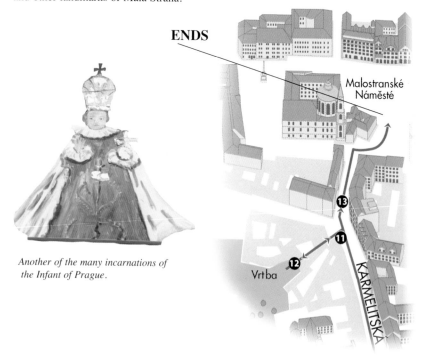

Another of the many incarnations of the Infant of Prague.

Left, the Vrtba Gardens are full of pretty features.

⑬ When you're done basking in the view, retrace your steps to Karmelitská, where a left turn and short walk will bring you to **Malostranské náměstí**, a nexus for many convenient tram connections. Or continue on to Charles Bridge for the 'Origins of a City' walk (page 26).

A dramatic pose from one of the many statues in the Vrtba Gardens.

Left, relax after a day's walking and discover Prague's thriving nightlife.

Myths and Legends: Vyšehrad Circuit

This is the seat of Czech legends, a rocky outcrop overlooking the Vltava where mythology and religion and dramatic geography combine to weave a spell that has enchanted generations of natives and visitors. It was from this site that Princess Libuše sent a magic horse (or human delegation, depending on who is telling the story) into the countryside to find Přemysl, a simple ploughman who became her husband and the founder of Prague's first ruling dynasty. Legend holds that Libuše looked across the river from this site to a forested hilltop and foresaw the founding of a great city whose glory would reach to the stars. Praha comes from the Czech word *práh*, meaning threshold.

The reality is rather more prosaic. Vyšehrad was originally the site of a 10thC fortress guarding the area from invasion from the south. It gained in importance when the Přemyslid princes, most notably Prince Vratislav II, built a palace there in the 10th century as a rival to Prague Castle. Later, it returned to its primary military purpose and was overrun and plundered during the Hussite wars. Most of the present-day layout and construction was done as part of the nationalist revival of the 19th century, when Vyšehrad was established as a national historic and cultural site.

RAŠÍNOVO NÁBŘEŽÍ

However, history takes a back seat when you wander this route's emerald pathways and towering brick ramparts, with their dramatic views of the river and Prague Castle. The ancient, mythical spirit of the place is still very much in the air, and, if allowed to work on your imagination, may well inspire magical visions of your own.

The view from Vyšehrad's battlements.

▶ **STARTS**
Vyšehrad metro stop

■ **ENDS**
Roman Basilica of St. Lawrence.
Nearest metro stop:
Vyšehrad.

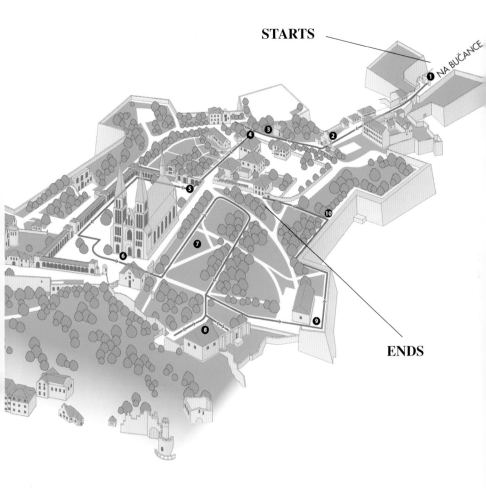

STARTS

NA BUČANCE

ENDS

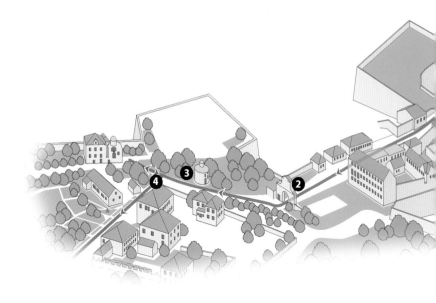

1 From the **Vyšehrad metro stop**, where the lower asphalt walk heading west turns into **Na Bučance**, make for the **Tábor Gate**. This marks the beginning of the **Barbakán**, Vyšehrad's low-lying entrance area. The rest of Vyšehrad is surrounded by insurmountable walls, but Barbakán, open to invasion from the south and east, had to be fortified with a series of gates. The name of the first gate is a reference to Tábor, a city to the south that was the Hussite base during the religious wars of the early 15th century.

2 A short walk along **V pevnosti** brings you to the formal entrance of the fortifications, the imposing **Leopold Gate**, built in 1670 by the Italian architect Carlo Lurago. The distinctive double-headed eagle at the top is the insignia of the Habsburg Empire. Film buffs with sharp memories may recall this gate making a brief appearance near the end of Miloš Forman's *Amadeus*.

3 Bear right and almost immediately you will see the circular **St Martin's Rotunda** (right), reputed to be the oldest intact Romanesque structure in Prague. Built in the 11th century, it served a number of functions over the centuries, including gunpowder storage. It is now a functioning (if tiny) chapel. Just beyond, you'll see the **Plague Pillar**, whose faces are as close as you will ever want to get to the real thing; and the **Chapel of the Virgin Mary On the Ramparts**. The building to which it is attached was once the colourfully-named **Church of the Decapitation of St. John the Baptist**.

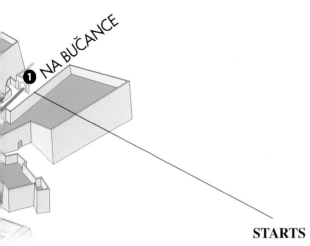

STARTS

Details from the Chapel of the Virgin Mary (above and top right).
Right, the Devil's Pillar.

❹ There are many paths and leafy nooks to explore in Vyšehrad, and if you continue past the Chapel of Decapitation on the same walkway you will reach the massive Brick Gate and discover nearby a lovely sculpture garden in the north-west corner of the park. This route,

however, turns instead on to **K Rotundé**, opposite St Martin's, and takes you towards the distinctive twin spires of **Sts Peter and Paul**. After you pass the **Canon's Residence** on your left, look in the grassy area to your right for the **Devil's Pillar**, a tripod of fat stone columns. There are several stories about how and why these slabs landed here. A mural painting in the northern lateral aisle inside the church shows a flying devil assisting the church's construction by bringing a column from Rome. Evidently he dropped it short of the mark.

Detail from St Leopold's Gate.

85

5 Immediately beyond the Devil's Pillar, a doorway in the stone wall leads to the stunning **Vyšehrad Cemetery**, where many of the nation's literary and cultural luminaries are buried. The centerpiece is **Slavín**, an elaborate monument and mausoleum for some of the brightest lights in the Bohemian heavenly firmament. See if you can find the nameplates for Art Nouveau master Alfons Mucha and sculptor J.V. Myslbek. Mylsbek created the statuary in the adjacent sculpture garden, through which you will soon wander. In the colonnade ringing the cemetery you'll find intricate tile mosaics, sculptures of angels in mourning, and the graves of some of the greatest names in Czech music and literature: Antonín Dvořák, Bedrich Smetana and Karel Čapek. The entire cemetery is effectively a sculpture garden, and well worth some time spent in aesthetic and spiritual contemplation.

Eclectic details from the cemetery.

6 Leaving the south-west corner of the cemetery nearest the church brings you to the front doors of **Sts Peter and Paul**. This elaborate, neo-Gothic basilica dates back to the 11th century, but it was expanded and refurbished many times. Much of the current interior decoration is from the early 1900s. The western face of the basilica alone is worth a look. (A restaurant directly opposite the church with outdoor tables in the summer offers one of the best vantage points.) Look for the detailed stone reliefs and mosaics above the doors, and the towering castellated spires. A small fee gets you inside, where it's often too dark to appreciate the rich murals covering almost every inch of wall and ceiling space, depicting subjects that

range from the establishment of Vyšehrad to the lives of the church's namesakes.

The exquisite lintel of the church door, far left. Left, detail from the door itself.

The armoury gate.

7 When you leave the front doors of the church, turn left and walk through the stone gate (the remnants of a Baroque armoury) into the **sculpture garden** – more like a field, really – where Myslbek's larger-than-life-size heroes of Czech mythology hold sway. There's Libuše and Přemysl (she's standing with her arm extended, he's sitting); Šárka the warrior with Ctirad, the lover whom she murdered (she's standing, he's kneeling); Záboj and Slavoj, who drove off the invading Franks (both standing, with weapons at the ready and a victory wreath extended); and the brave bard Lumír with the muse Song. Follow the route as marked.

Záboj and Slavoj.

8 Now you're about to walk the ramparts, where great deeds were performed and visionaries foresaw the future. You will see two observation points a short distance south-west of the sculpture garden. The smaller, reached through a doorway, looks down on to **Libuše's Bath**, actually the remains of a 14thC watch tower. The ruin also marks the point where the legendary horse Semik jumped into the Vltava, saving the life of his master and rider, Horymir. The larger observation point offers a majestic view of the river and Prague Castle. A brass relief plate identifies the bridges and other visible landmarks. Between the two, a

small **art gallery** features exhibitions of contemporary Czech art.

9 Follow the rampart wall to the south and almost immediately you will come to one of the best vantage points in Vyšehrad, the south-west battlement, where an observation deck offers a sweeping view south. This is the real Prague laid out before you, a city of red-tiled roofs punctuated by church steeples with boatyards and marinas and railway bridges lining the Vltava River as it winds its way north to merge with the Elbe. Here you can also get a sense of what Czech composer Bedrich Smetana had in mind

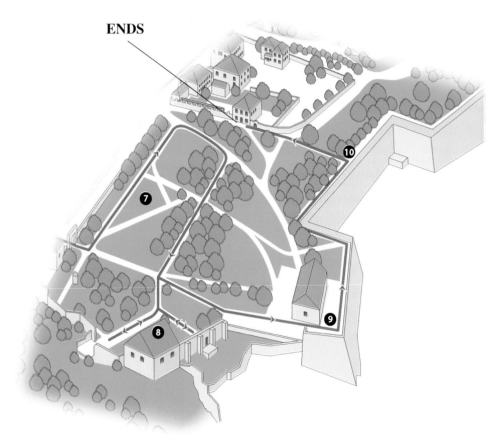

ENDS

when he composed *Má Vlast* (My Country), one of his most famous works and a cultural touchstone for the Czechs. The first movement, Vyšehrad, opens with the sounds of Lumír's harp and goes on to describe the rise and fall of the original castle which stood on the site. The second movement, Vltava, follows the river from its source in the Šumava mountains through forests and fields, past a farmer's wedding and mermaids dancing, over tumbling rapids and finally past Vyšehrad and through Prague.

⑩ If you continue to follow the rampart wall to the east, a ten-minute walk brings you back to the entrance gate. Or do some exploring and playing along the way. The first walkway to your left drops down a set of stairs to the **Old Deanery** and what's left of the **Roman Basilica of St Lawrence**, where you can relax in a shaded café over coffee or a cold Czech beer. Further along the rampart wall, an unmarked play area offers some clever gymnastic challenges for the kids.

Or just wander. Vyšehrad is not big enough to get lost in, but its winding pathways, monuments and meticulously restored buildings offer many possibilities for exploration.

Top, above and right, breathtaking views from observation points along this part of the walk. Top, Libuše's Bath.

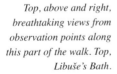

Luxurious palaces, charming lanes, red roofs: Malá Strana

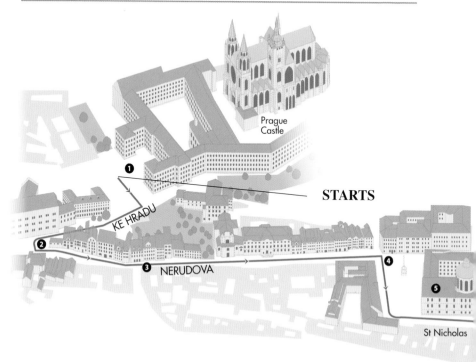

Prague
Castle

STARTS

KE HRADU

NERUDOVA

St Nicholas

Of all the neighbourhoods in Prague, Malá Strana is the one that most captivates visitors. Everyone is charmed by its sea of red-tiled roofs, quiet back lanes, luxurious palaces and the regal atmosphere of embassies and stately government offices that somehow blends in seamlessly with the usual mix of pubs, restaurants and souvenir shops. While other areas of the city have given themselves over to commerce and commercialism, Malá Strana keeps its own counsel, remaining serene and mysterious even as tourists pour down its central artery, Nerudova street.

The area was formally established as a town in 1257, then grew rapidly during the reign of Charles IV, who enlarged it and built fortifications. Two great fires burned through the area in the 16th century, giving rise to a new aristocracy in the shadow of the Castle and a wealth of magnificent churches. Baroque was the reigning architectural style, reaching its apotheosis in the stunning work by three generations of the Dientzenhofer family on St Nicholas Church. When the centre of political power moved to Vienna in the 17th century, the nobility left and the neighbourhood reverted to craftsmen

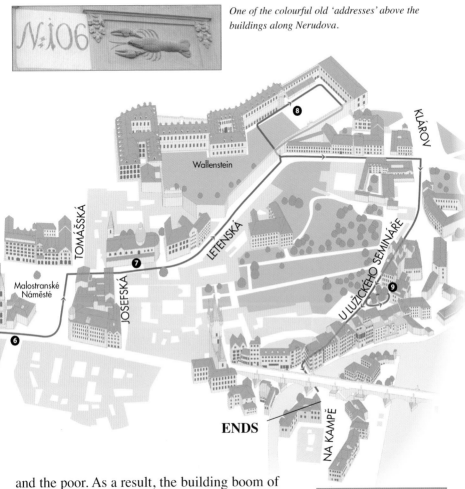

One of the colourful old 'addresses' above the buildings along Nerudova.

and the poor. As a result, the building boom of the 19th and 20th centuries passed it by, helping shape the neighbourhood's unique character.

This is another great area for exploring stairways, alleys and side-streets just to see where they go. The same is true for intriguing doorways. What appears to be a small place from the street can open into a large subterranean space inside. Prague doesn't give up its secrets easily, and that's true here more than anywhere else in the city. There's no telling what you'll find.

▶ STARTS
Malá Strana. Nearest metro stop: Malostranská. Take tram 22 to either Pražský hrad or Pohořelec.

■ ENDS
Charles Bridge. Nearest metro stop: Malostranská.

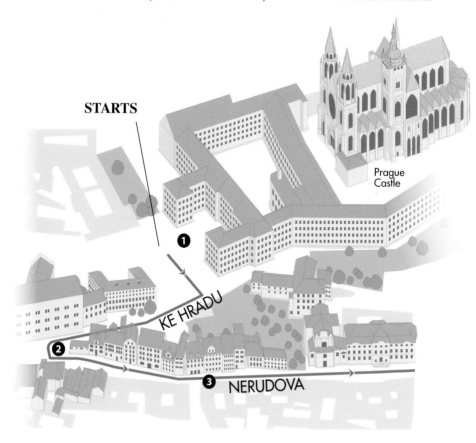

STARTS

Prague
Castle

❶ Our starting point is the **Malá Strana overlook** at **Prague Castle**, located just south (to the right) of the **main gate**. A cascade of red-tiled roofs drops to the spires and domes of St Nicholas and the Church of Our Lady Victorious, and beyond, the geography and landmarks of the eastern half of the city are visible across the Vltava. The tall, needle-like structure on the horizon is the Žižkov TV tower, a futuristic communist monstrosity built in the 1980s on top of a Jewish cemetery. If you have time to explore that part of the city, it's worth a trip to the base of the tower to gape up at what seems to be a rocket about to explode into space. The faceless baby sculptures crawling around the upper reaches of the tower are the work of art prankster David Černý.

❷ Drop to your right down the short cobble-stoned length of **Ke Hradu**, which will bring you to the base of an opposing stairway. A quick hairpin turn to your left

A dramatic sky hangs over the city: the view from Hradčanské náměstí.

puts you on **Nerudova**, where the first thing you will see is a plaque commemorating an ugly incident that happened in early 1948. Students marching against the new communist regime were attacked and beaten by the police: a harbinger of 40 years of oppression that lay ahead. It's a disconcerting note in an otherwise pleasant setting, but a useful reminder that freedom is never easily won.

Clockwise from top left: an eagle guards the Italian Embassy; a Moor shoulders the Romanian Embassy; detail from Jan Neruda's house; two of the colourful symbols on Nerudova; and an irreverent restaurant.

❸ Nerudova has an appealing mix of shops and restaurants, but the chief attraction is the curious set of symbols over many of the doorways, which at one time had a practical function: they served as addresses before numbers were introduced in 1770. The poet Jan Neruda, the namesake for the street, lived at **no. 47,** the **House of Two Suns.** The **House of the Green Crayfish (no. 43)** is now appropriately a restaurant; the **Golden Horseshoe (no. 34)** was once a pharmacy; the **House of Three Fiddles (no. 12)** was the home of a violin-maker. The Italian architect Giovanni Santini, who worked on many projects in Malá Strana in the early 1700s, designed two buildings on the street that are now embassies: **Thun Hohenstein Palace (no. 20)**, with the fierce eagles guarding the door, is the Italian embassy, and **Morzin Palace (no. 5)**, where a pair of Moors carry the balcony on their backs, is the Romanian embassy.

❹ At the bottom of the hill, Nerudova opens into **Malostranské náměstí**, a large square that encompasses both sides of **St Nicholas Church**. At the centre of the upper square, a plague column – yet another erected in thanksgiving by survivors of the plague – is distinctive in having the Holy Trinity at the top, a spot usually reserved for the Virgin Mary. On the west side of the square, **Lichtenstein Palace (no. 13)** was once the home of Karel of Lichtenstein, known as 'bloody Lichtenstein' for sentencing to death the 27 leaders of the Estates uprising in 1621. The execution was done in Old Town Square but the sentencing took place here, an act commemorated by 27 cast-iron heads mounted on a row of posts in front of the building. Used since as a post office and military barracks, Lichtenstein Palace today houses the music school of Prague's Academy of Performing Arts, whose students and faculty put on excellent classical music concerts at very reasonable prices. Check the programmes inside the lobby.

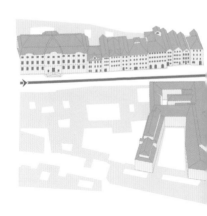

❺ The upper square is dominated by St Nicholas Church, the Baroque counterpart to the Gothic wonder of St Vitus Cathedral. Though considerably smaller in size, St Nicholas gives away nothing in grandeur, with the enormous fresco depicting the life of St Nicholas

Lichtenstein Palace.

that covers the ceiling reputed to be one of the largest in Europe. The main nave was built by Krzštof Dientzenhofer between 1703 and 1711. His son Kilián Ignác put on the dome 25 years later, and Kilián's son-in-law Anselmo Lurago added the bell tower between 1751 and 1756. The interior is a riot of statuary, frescoes and gilded side altars, as if Hieronymus Bosch had decided to paint heaven instead of hell. Mozart played the organ here, and after his death in December 1791, throngs of Praguers packed the church for a memorial service.

A quirky bollard in Malostranské náměstí.

The courtyard of the Lichtenstein Palace.

Baroque St Nicholas Church.

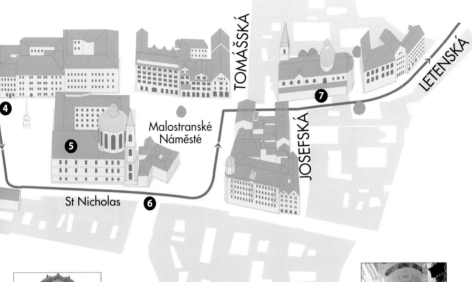

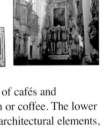

Left, the exterior of St Thomas. Right, the distinctive red street sign for Tomášská. Far right, St Thomas's impressive altar.

6 Walking around the south side of St Nicholas will take you past a row of cafés and restaurants tucked under a colonnade, a convenient place to stop for lunch or coffee. The lower part of Malostranské náměstí offers a blend of Renaissance and Baroque architectural elements, the result of the 16th century fires, which roared through on the cusp of the two styles. The juxtaposition is evident in separate buildings – **no. 22** is Renaissance, **no. 23** is Baroque – and even in single buildings, most prominently the one facing the square at the corner of **Tomášská street (Tomášská no. 1)**. It has Renaissance-style archways, windows and *sgraffito*, topped by a Baroque pediment. The long building on the upper part of the square (attached to St Nicholas, though it's difficult to see from here) was built by the Jesuits as a college for priests. It now houses the mathematics department of Charles University.

7 Walk through the square and leave it to the east on **Letenská**, which will take you past two lesser-known but lovely churches. Almost immediately to your left, you will see **St Thomas**, which was founded by the Order of Augustinian Hermits in 1285. Successive improvements and additions included a monastery and brewery, and a major Baroque makeover by the Dientzenhofer clan during the 1720s. If the church is open, you can see one of the most impressive choir lofts in the city, and copies of two paintings by Rubens flanking the main altar (the originals are in the National Gallery collection). On **Josefská**, a side-street to the right, **St Joseph** is noteworthy for its tall columnar frontispiece, which combines Dutch and Italian elements.

8 Continue along Letenská – carefully. The traffic along this narrow stretch (including trams) doesn't slow down for pedestrians. However, Letenská is the best way to reach the remarkable

Crowds gather for a concert inside Wallenstein Gardens.

Wallenstein Gardens (closed in winter). Look for the dimunitive doorway on the left (west) side where the street bends. A mid-17th century ego exercise by the military commander Albrecht of Wallenstein, the formal gardens include fountains, an aviary (usually stocked with owls) and a bizarre 'grotto wall' that looks like it was lifted from an underground cavern. The mythological statuary is all copies of the originals, which the Swedes made off with in 1648. (A few years ago, the Czechs officially asked the Swedes to return them; the Swedes laughed and declined.) The west end of the gardens is dominated by an enormous triple-arched *sala terrena*, where concerts are held in summer. A doorway to the right (north) of the stage may or may not be open, providing access to **Wallenstein Palace**, a massive late Renaissance-early Baroque complex built by Albrecht to rival Prague Castle. He demolished 23 houses to make room for it, hired the best Italian architects money could buy to design and build it, and employed a staff of 700 to run it. Today the Palace houses the administrative offices of the Czech Parliament.

9 Leave the gardens where you came in, continuing along Letenská, and turn right at the first corner on to **U Ležického Semináře**. When the street forks, bear to your left on to

Cihelná, which will bring you to the **Kafka Museum**. Museum and gift shop are worth a stop, though many people get no further than the sculpture out front of two men peeing in a fountain. It's startling and funny all at once, though can be frightening for small children. Blame David Černý, the art provocateur who put St Wenceslas on an upside-down horse in Lucerna and babies on the TV tower.

David Černý's provocative sculpture.

10 When you leave the Kafka Museum, turn left, which will take you through a small triangular park back to U Ležického Semináře. Along the way, look on your left for **Shakespeare and Sons (no. 10)**, the best English-language bookstore in the city. The next left brings you to a small bridge over **Čertovká creek**, from which you have several options. You can continue along U Ležického Semináře, and then Mostecká, back to Malostranské náměstí, which has a number of tram connections. Or you can start one of the other walks from this point. Walking under Charles Bridge will bring you to Na Kampě, the starting point for the 'Riverfront Walk' (page 98). Or take the stairway up on to the bridge to begin 'Charles Bridge to Old Town Square' (page 26).

The small park leading on to U Ležického Semináře.

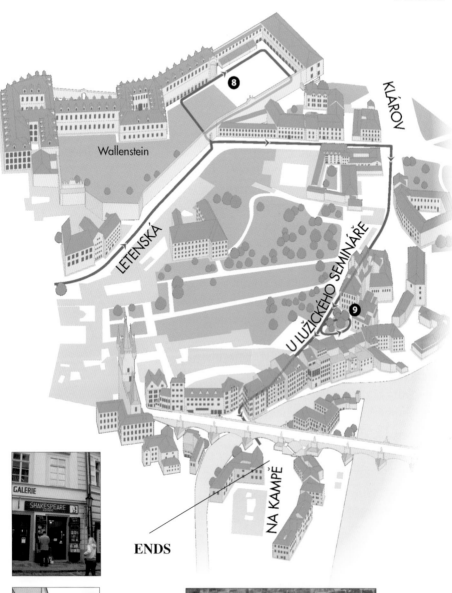

KLÁROV

Wallenstein

LETENSKÁ

U LUŽICKÉHO SEMINÁŘE

8

9

NA KAMPĚ

ENDS

*Above,
Shakespeare
and Sons.
Left,
Čertovká
Creek.*

*Your walk
ends here,
under
Charles
Bridge.*

Riverfront Walk: From Kampa Park to Karlovo náměstí

No city walking guide is complete without a river front route. Prague has not been very good about making its riverfront accommodating to visitors, though locals will tell you it's much more inviting now than it was during the communist era, when dirty grey buildings loomed along unlit banks. There's plenty of light now, along with bright, freshly painted façades and expensive restaurants, where you can dine literally in the shadow of the Charles Bridge.

For energetic sightseers wanting to spend an afternoon on the river (instead of a fortune), this walk through the central part of the city takes in both contemporary and historic points of interest. The riverfront also offers some of the city's best vantage points, especially at night, when the bridges are lit and landmarks such as Prague Castle and the National Theatre glow like a pastel-coloured dream on the skyline.

Keep your eyes peeled for details such as these grinning faces in Masarykovo nábřeží.

▶ **STARTS**
Na Kampě.
Nearest metro stop:
Malostranská.

■ **ENDS**
Karlovo náměstí.
Nearest metro stop:
Karlovo náměstí.

The Vltava River (*Moldau* in German) is the largest in the Czech Republic, flowing nearly 270 miles (435 km) as it winds from its source in the Šumava mountains in the south to Mělník, north of Prague, where it joins the Labe River (Elbe in German). During summer months, the Prague portion of the river is a beehive of activity, filled with noisy tour boats, rental rowboats and peddle boats, as well as flocks of seagulls and waterfowl. The Vltava made international headlines in August 2002, when after weeks of heavy rainfall it overflowed and flooded parts of Prague, causing heavy damage. Most of the damage has been repaired, but some markers along this route will give you an idea of how devastating it was.

Or you might spot this much more sombre face, also in Masarykovo nábřeží.

MOST LEGIÍ

RELECKÝ ÓSTROV

SLOVANSKÝ OSTROV

RESSLOVA

KARLOVO NÁMĚSTÍ

ENDS

Malá
Strana

Exhibit from the sculpture garden in the Museum Kampa.

STARTS

❶ Start at **Na Kampě**, the main square of **Kampa Island**. It sits below the west end of **Charles Bridge**, accessible via a stone staircase (*right*), whose entrance is between the statues of St Luitgarda (having a vision of Christ on the cross) and St Nicholas of Tolentino (handing out bread to the poor). In the 19th century this was a well-known pick-up spot, with prostitutes in the square soliciting customers for business in the surrounding buildings. Today the twin rows of pastel-coloured buildings house offices, restaurants and cafés, and, on the far right-hand side, the Estonian Embassy. After the bustling, noisy crowds on the bridge, here is a subdued spot to rest on the benches or do some people watching over coffee at one of the outdoor cafés.

Left, a row of pastel houses in Na Kampě. Above, can you spot this charming detail?

The view from Na Kampě.

The enormous židle.

2 Walking through the square brings you directly into Kampa Park, a small but pleasant patch of greenery shaded by towering chestnut trees. If the weather is nice, the grass will be covered with sunbathers and people playing with their dogs. Instead of threading your way through them, an immediate left will bring you to a wall that runs along the riverbank. There are some charming views of the river and Charles Bridge as you follow the wall to Museum Kampa, where the path takes a sharp right. Here, look at the embankment wall, where you will see a large wooden sculpture called *židle* (chair). The original, much smaller version, was swept away in the 2002 flood. This one is not going anywhere – come hell or high water.

The Kampa museum hosts a variety of worthwhile exhibitions.

3 The right turn and then an immediate left bring you to the entrance of **Museum Kampa**, one of the city's most interesting arts institutions. Originally a flour mill, the building was gutted and reconstructed in the early 2000s to house the collection of Jan and Mleda Mládek, Czech emigrés who spent much of their lives in exile, working in Washington. During this period, Jan became one of the first governors of the International Monetary Fund and together they collected major works by Czech and other Central European artists, in particular painter František Kupka, collagist Jiří Kolář and sculptor Otto Gutfreund. The museum also mounts shows by popular 20thC artists such as Andy Warhol and Yoko Ono. It's definitely worth a visit if you have the time. If not, be sure to stroll through the courtyard, which has a café and sculpture garden, noting that the floodwaters rose 6 m high against these walls.

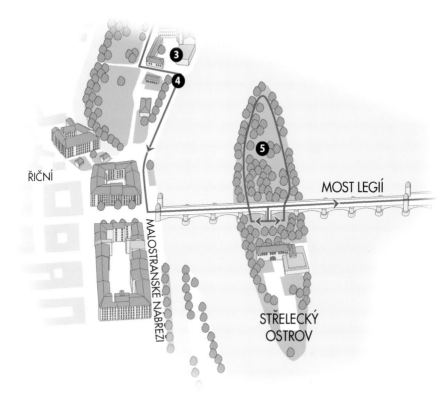

ŘIČNÍ

MOST LEGIÍ

MALOSTRANSKÉ NÁBŘEŽÍ

STŘELECKÝ
OSTROV

*Colourful posters on
Říční street, above.
Right, ornamental
stonework on a lamp
post on Most Legií.*

4 Leaving by the other side of the courtyard brings you a vantage point for admiring more sculptures, river views and ducks looking for a handout. Continue south along the river, following the wall on your right, which was destroyed by the flood and has since been rebuilt. This will bring you to **Říční street**, where a stone staircase leads up to a short walk along tree-lined **Malostranské nábřeží**. Turn left on to **Most Legií** (Legionnaire's Bridge). There is some fine ornamental stonework at either end of the bridge, and at the base of the lamp posts along the bridge, but the principal attraction is the view, particularly after dark. There is no single better shot of Prague Castle than from this bridge at night, when it hovers like a pastel-colored cloud on the skyline.

Pick up an unusual gift on Malostranské nábřeží.

The view from Most Legií.

⑤ Most Legií also gives you access to the island below — look for the stone staircase to your right about halfway across the bridge. **Střelecký Ostrov** (Sharpshooter's Island) is a green oasis in the middle of the city, with plenty of shady trees and benches lining the shoreline. Take a stroll to the north end of the island, where anglers can usually be found, for a panoramic view of Charles Bridge and both sides of the river. During the flood, you could not have done this; the island was completely submerged, with the water rising to just a metre or so below the

Above, the steps into Střelecký Ostrov, and left, the lovely view from the tranquil island.

bridge. This barely stopped the open-air cinema that was running on the island that summer, which continued nightly screenings of films such as The Rocky Horror Picture Show even as the water was lapping at the disappearing banks. The cinema was very popular, with live music performances as well. Sadly as we went to press, the cinema's future was in doubt, and there was no summer cinema and music program scheduled.

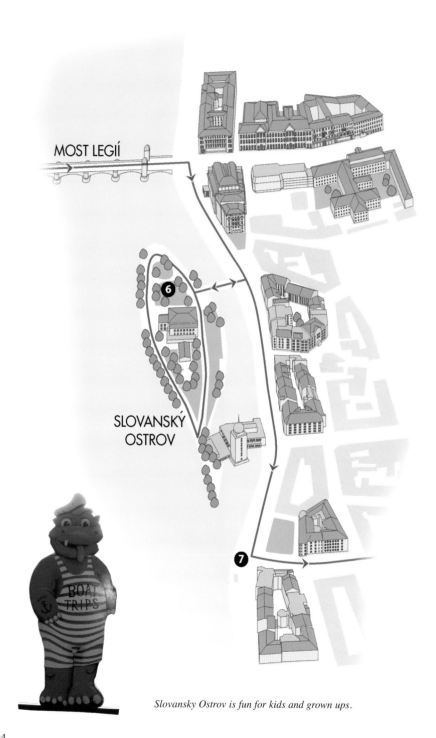

MOST LEGIÍ

6

SLOVANSKÝ
OSTROV

7

BOAT
TRIPS

Slovansky Ostrov is fun for kids and grown ups.

Neo-Renaissance Žofín.

Contemporary art gallery Mánes.

6 Retrace your steps to Most Legií , continuing to the other side, then, after you've crossed the bridge, take a right and follow the river south, past the **National Theatre** (the starting point for the 'New Town' walk, page 118) to the small bridge on your right that connects to **Slovansky Ostrov** (Slavonic Island). More commercial than Střelecký, here you can rent rowboats and peddle boats during the summer, another enjoyable way to pass a hot day. The centrepiece of the island is the stately neo-Renaissance **Žofín** building, a social and cultural centre used mostly for private balls, receptions and business events. Unfortunately, that means you probably won't get to see the sumptuous interior, although you can stop for a beer or coffee on the outdoor terrace. Beyond that you'll find a children's playground and, at the southern tip of the island, **Galerie Mánes**, a contemporary art gallery named for the 19th-century Czech painter Josef Mánes. The striking functionalist building also houses a restaurant and dance club.

7 Return to the river bank, across the bridge where you entered, a three-block walk south will bring you to the corner of **Resslova Street**, where you cannot miss the famous **Dancing Building**. Also known as 'Fred and Ginger' for its suggestion of dancing partners, this was the product of a collaboration between Czech architect Vlado Milunic and American architect Frank Gehry. It was a radical building at the time it was completed in 1996, but now seems tame compared with much of Gehry's recent work, such as the Guggenheim Museum in Bilbao. Gehry has said in interviews that the design for the Dancing Building came from the architects not wanting to interfere with a neighbour's view of Prague Castle.

'Fred and Ginger', the Dancing Building.

The Cathedral of Sts Cyril and Methodius.

8 Turn left on to **Resslova**, which is not a very pedestrian-friendly street, but worth braving for a couple blocks to get to the imposing **Cathedral of Sts Cyril and Methodius**, where the final scene of one of the great dramas of the Second World War took place. On May 27, 1942, two Czech soldiers staged an assassination attempt against Nazi commander Reinhard Heydrich, Reichsprotektor of Bohemia and Moravia. Heydrich was wounded and died several days later; meanwhile, the two soldiers fled and eventually hid in the crypt of this church. They were discovered, and on June 18, the cathedral was surrounded by hundreds of German soldiers. The assassins held out for nearly 24 hours, but were finally overwhelmed and used their last final bullets to take their own lives. The story is recounted in a dramatic display in the crypt of the church, where the men made their last stand.

Busy Resslova, left, and the distinctive red sign for Karlovo náměstí, above.

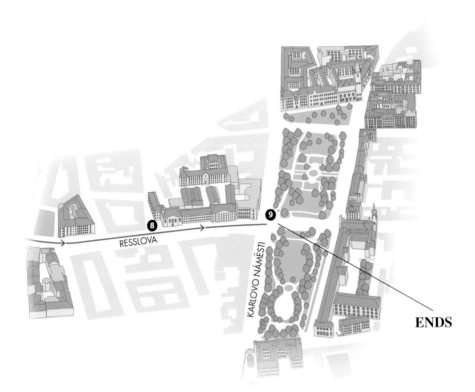

ENDS

9 Continuing along Resslova will bring you to **Karlovo náměstí**, where you'll find connections for many trams and the Metro B (yellow) line. Catch either the number 6 or 22 tram at the northeast corner of Resslova and Spálená (at the edge of the park) and a ride of two stops will bring you to the National Theatre, the starting point for the 'New Town' walk (page 118).

Memorial for the two assassins, in the Cathedral of Sts Cyril and Methodius – see **8***.*

Communist Relics: Florence to Wenceslas Square

The striking sculptural façade of no.24, Na Poříčí.

This is the road less-travelled in Prague, the forgotten part of city centre - at least for visitors. It's easy to see why, with the stunning architecture of Old Town ending at náměstí Republiky and the streets beyond quickly winding into a workaday maze. But there are some gems on this eastern side of New Town, and it is arguably a more accurate representation of the contrasts between modern and Communist Prague than the more visited areas surrounding it.

In that sense, this area is a measure of how far Prague has come since the Velvet Revolution, with bastions of capitalism towering regally over decrepit remnants of the communist era. There are echoes of an earlier Prague here as well – much earlier, going back to prehistoric times, and more recently during the golden era between the world wars, when Czechoslovakia was one of the great economic powers and literary centres of Europe.

There's a sadness in seeing places frozen in time, a sense of loss in realizing what might have been had the country not suffered under 50 years of tyranny and neglect. But there's also hope, not just in the modern shops and hotels, but in the bits of art, culture and commerce that flourished even in dark times. Modest though they may be, they are triumphs of the human spirit. And even the 20thC tyrants respected tradition, leaving key historic and religious sites intact.

ENDS

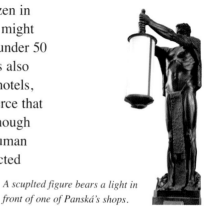

A scuplted figure bears a light in front of one of Panská's shops.

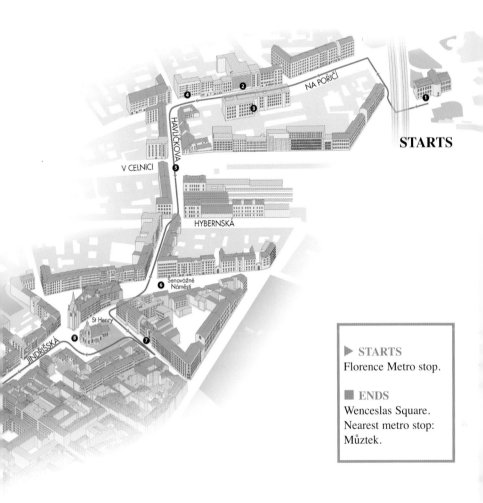

NA POŘÍČÍ

HAVLÍČKOVA

V CELNICI

HYBERNSKÁ

Senovážné
Náměstí

St Henry

JINDŘIŠSKÁ

STARTS

▶ **STARTS**
Florence Metro stop.

■ **ENDS**
Wenceslas Square.
Nearest metro stop:
Můztek.

*Art Deco detail from the
amazing Café Imperial.*

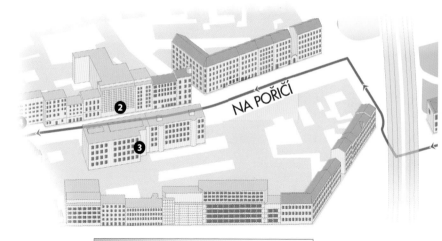

1 The **Florence metro stop** is the hub of the area and affords convenient access to the **Prague City Museum**, an imposing neo-Renaissance structure built in the late 1800s. In terms of fine art, the museum offers a modest collection ranging from furnishings to religious artefacts.

Prague City Museum and one of its many exhibits (below).

But there is no better place in the city to get a sense of how Prague has developed from ancient times, especially with all the exhibits being labelled in both Czech and English. And there are some great curiosities, starting in the lobby with a zodiac face made by Josef Mánes in the mid 1800s for the Old Town Square astronomical clock. Don't miss the remarkable scale model of Prague on the second floor, which offers an unparalleled overview of the city with special lighting to highlight the historic areas.

2 **Na Poříčí** was built along an old trade route, and as you walk along it you will see the most ubiquitous hallmarks of modern commerce - fast food restaurants such as McDonald's and KFC, which tend to be among the busier spots on the street. One of the last living vestiges of the Communist era is at **no. 23: Bílá Labut'** (White Swan), a socialist department store. A stroll through this is like a visit to bygone era, with sullen clerks looking suspiciously out from behind cases of oddly juxtaposed goods: handbags stacked next to bicycles, cheap nylon stockings just a couple of steps down from the pastries. If you're in the area after dark, look for the giant neon swan that spins atop the building.

The White Swan sign of the socialist department store – see ❷*.*

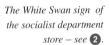

STARTS

❸ Across the street are two buildings worthy of note, both former offices of the Ministry of Industry. The passage at **no. 26** is the entrance to **Divadlo Archa**, Prague's finest avant-garde space for contemporary theatre, dance and music. It occupies what was formerly the E.F. Burian Theatre, named after the great director, composer and playwright who ran one of Europe's most influential leftist theatre operations on that site in the years between the world wars. Next door, **no. 24** is now a bank, with one of the most arresting sculptural façades in the city, an amalgam of labourers and soldiers that celebrates work and war, with one of the prominent figures clad in a gas mask.

The bank at no.24.

Above and right, the arresting exterior and interior of the bank.

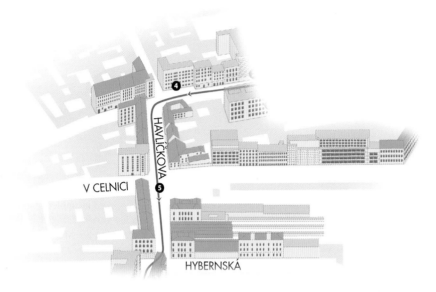

❹ A few steps further down the block, the **Café Imperial** (*right*) is worth a stop, if not for coffee or lunch, then just to see the eye-popping ornamental plasterwork and tile mosaics that cover the columns, walls and ceilings. The Art Deco café and adjoining hotel are much less shabby since a 2007 refurbishment, though certainly not up to the five-star billing the hotel has conferred upon itself. Sadly, the café recently abandoned a unique and long-standing tradition: on your birthday, you and your friends could buy a plate of day-old doughnuts and throw them at each other, just like a school canteen food fight. If you dine there be sure to check your bill, as the Café Imperial staff are notorious for overcharging tourists for a few extra crowns.

❺ Turn left on **Havlíčkova** and for a few blocks you will get a mini-tour of old and new Prague. On the cross-street **V Celnici** there are modern American hotels and an upmarket shopping mall done up in glass and chrome, while just past **V Celnici**, it's hard to imagine what is holding up the crumbling **Masarykovo nádraží** (Masaryk train station). It's the oldest station in Prague – the first train arrived in August, 1845 – and

The view down Havlickova.

shows its age. Masarykovo nádraží is emblematic of the condition of most train stations throughout the country, which the state-owned railway line has been trying for years to lease to private companies (without much success) for refurbishment and retail rejuvenation. Continue along the next block, crossing **Hybernská**, where the road turns into **Dlažděná**, once known as 'book collectors' row'. Reconstruction has driven away most of the bookshops, with just two sad *antikvariats* (antique or secondhand shops) remaining. But they're worth a stop if you fancy vintage posters and postcards.

An eye-catching antique bookshop.

The intricate interior of Art Deco style Cafe Imperial.

The interior of the oldest station in Prague.

Senovážná náměstí.

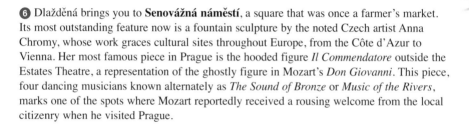

❻ Dlažděná brings you to **Senovážná náměstí**, a square that was once a farmer's market. Its most outstanding feature now is a fountain sculpture by the noted Czech artist Anna Chromy, whose work graces cultural sites throughout Europe, from the Côte d'Azur to Vienna. Her most famous piece in Prague is the hooded figure *Il Commendatore* outside the Estates Theatre, a representation of the ghostly figure in Mozart's *Don Giovanni*. This piece, four dancing musicians known alternately as *The Sound of Bronze* or *Music of the Rivers*, marks one of the spots where Mozart reportedly received a rousing welcome from the local citizenry when he visited Prague.

❼ Exiting the square to your right and continuing along what turns into **Jindřišská street** will bring you to the first cross street, **Jeruzalémská**. Turn left and within a block you will see one of the city's most distinctive pieces of architecture, the **Jerusalem Synagogue** (also

Anna Chromy's graceful fountain sculpture.

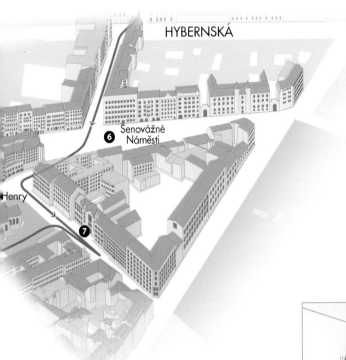

HYBERNSKÁ

Senovážné
Náměsti

Henry

known as the Jubilee Synagogue). After the late-19thC razing of Prague's Jewish Quarter destroyed three synagogues, a group of worshippers purchased this site in 1899 and commissioned a design for a new synagogue by the renowned Viennese architect Wilhelm Stiassny. The façade features a Moorish Art Nouveau treatment, extended in the deep interior space

Jindrisská street.

The ornate exterior of the Jubilee Synagogue.

with twin rows of seven Islamic arches. The synagogue survived the Second World War by virtue of being used as a warehouse, and is aglow now with a loving restoration that began in 1992 and took nearly 15 years to complete.

8 From the synagogue, a paved way cuts through the small triangular park that leads you back to Jindřišská street and the **Church of St Jindřicha** (St Henry) **and Kunhuta** (his wife). This was one of the first parish churches established in Prague, built in 1351. It has been refurbished many times since, with a complete Gothic makeover in the 1870s. Directly across the street is the church bell tower, built in the 1570s. It's taken quite a beating over the centuries: during the Swedish invasion of 1648 it was attacked when Bohemian snipers took refuge there, and in 1801 a storm blew the roof off the tower. It stands strong today though, with a 20thC bank building attached and a small souvenir shop and café inside.

9 Continuing along Jindřišská brings you back toward the commercial centre of the city, with two appropriate stops. Turn right at **Panská** for the **Mucha Museum**, a well-appointed tribute to the Art Nouveau master Alfons Mucha. With so

The Church of St Jindřišská, and the bell tower directly across the street (right).

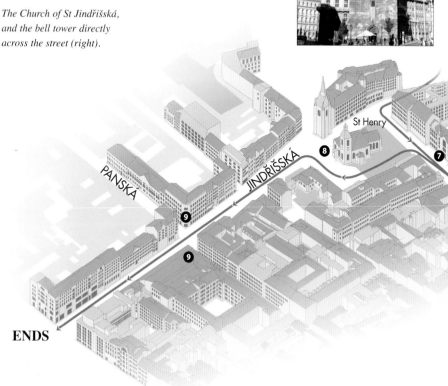

much of Mucha's work on display in other parts of the city, you may want to skip the museum proper, which is expensive. However, the gift shop is excellent, with Mucha and Prague's other cultural icon, Franz Kafka, on mugs, t-shirts, scarves, posters and even some classy souvenir items. A few steps further along Jindřišská you will see the mammoth **Česká Poštá**, the main post office. Even if you have nothing to mail, it's worth a stop inside to see the elaborate *sgraffito* ringing the main hall. Then another half-block's walk down **Jindřišská** will bring you to **Wenceslas Square**.

The Mucha Museum gift shop, full of Mucha- and Kafka-themed souvenirs, above and right.

The stylish interior of the main post office.

New Town: National Theatre to the Botanical Gardens

The cliché about New Town is that it's neither. Created in the 14th century when Charles IV expanded Prague's increasingly crowded residences and fortifications, it's hardly new, and there's little now to distinguish it as a separate town. But it's the quarter of the city that best embodies Prague's emerging identity, encompassing historical sites, remnants of the communist era and the commerce and vibrancy of modern-day European life. New Town originally covered about 350 hectares, a greater area than Old

Detail from New Town Hall.

Town, Malá Strana and Hradčany combined. One of Charles's aims in establishing it was to get the noisy crafts and trades out of Old Town, and away from the newly established university. New Town thus became a flourishing production and trade centre, as well as a place inhabited by the working classes and poorer citizens. This gave it a radical character that came to the fore during the Hussite uprising of the early 15th century.

Today, New Town is predominantly a commercial district, with important historical and cultural anchors scattered throughout. Wenceslas Square (see page 42) is generally considered to be the heart of the area, and is a magnet for tourists. This walk and another one in New Town (see page 108) will take you through some less-travelled areas of its eastern and western flanks, revealing urban patchworks where glittery new shops and buildings rub shoulders with edifices still covered in centuries worth of grime.

Soldiers stand guard outside the children's theatre.

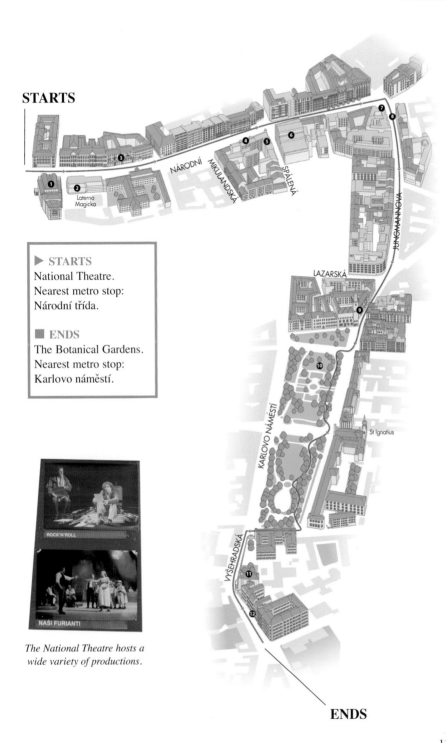

STARTS

ENDS

▶ **STARTS**
National Theatre.
Nearest metro stop:
Národní třída.

■ **ENDS**
The Botanical Gardens.
Nearest metro stop:
Karlovo náměstí.

*The National Theatre hosts a
wide variety of productions.*

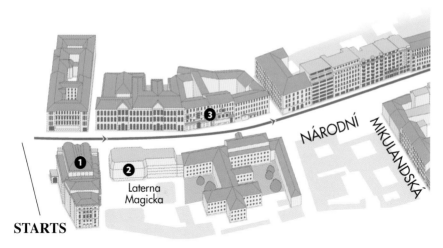

Laterna
Magicka

STARTS

Slavnostní
koncert

❶ The **National Theatre**, which stands proudly on the eastern bank of the Vltava River, is the cultural cornerstone of the nation. It was originally built in 1881, but not long after the inaugural performance (of Smetana's opera *Libuše*), the building burned to the ground. An extraordinary outpouring of public donations funded a complete rebuilding, which was completed within two years. Many of the country's finest artists of the era added the finishing touches, from the richly detailed murals in the main foyer to the horse-drawn chariots that top the façade. The theatre offers a rotating schedule of plays, opera and ballet, and it's definitely worth taking in a performance, if only to bask in the splendour of the regal auditorium.

❷ If the National Theatre is a stunning example of the right way to build a theatre, the frosted glass-lined **Laterna Magicka**, immediately next door, is just the opposite, a garish communist showpiece built in the late 1970s. The interior is done almost entirely in expensive marble and leather, both of which lost their lustre long ago. Along with black-light productions aimed primarily at tourists, the theatre hosts avant-garde drama and dance performances. For a more edifying experience, walk directly across the street to the **Czech Academy of Sciences** (at **no. 3**), a mid-19thC neo-Renaissance building that was originally a bank. Inside there's an impressive pair of stone lions guarding the entrance, and in the library beyond, marvellous sculptures overlooking the stacks.

The bizarre exterior of the Lanterna Magicka.

3 Exit the Academy, and continue eastwards along **Národní**. As you walk down, you'll see two adjoining buildings on the north side of the street that offer fine examples of late 19th/early 20thC architecture. Amid the relief sculptures that adorn **no. 7**, look for the word *pojištuje*, an indication that this was once an insurance company. The windows along the top spell out *Praha*. The Art Nouveau building next door, at **no. 9**, was once a publishing house. Directly opposite, on the south side of the street, a statue of St John Nepomuk stands in front of an **Ursuline convent**. Marked by a halo of stars, St John is a ubiquitous figure in Prague (his tomb is in St Vitus Cathedral and a prominent statue of him is on the Charles Bridge), and the subject of a great legend. Ordered by a Bohemian king to disclose a confession made to the priest by the queen, he refused, for which he was tortured and then thrown into the river. A ring of stars that later appeared over the river marked the spot where his body was recovered.

One of the lovely buildings along Národní.

Ornamental lintel of the National Theatre.

The sumptuous interior of the National Theatre.

St John Nepomuk.

121

4 Continue down the street, and after you cross **Mikulandská street**, walk through the colonnade on the south side of Národní where you will see a plaque marking the incident that sparked the Velvet Revolution. On November 17 1989, thousands of students chanting anti-communist slogans were confronted near this spot by riot police, who beat them and broke up the demonstration. Though no one died, word spread that a student had been killed. Massive strikes followed, and a week later 300,000 people gathered on Wenceslas Square to hear former Communist party leader Alexander Dubček and Civic Forum leader Václav Havel declare an end to communist rule. With the whole world watching on television and the Berlin Wall in ruins, the Soviets had little choice but to pack up and leave.

5 Just beyond the collonade, at **no. 22**, you'll see pictures of Havel in his halcyon days as Czech president with another luminary of the 1990s, United States President Bill Clinton. The photos are posted at the entrance to jazz club **Reduta**, where the two men enjoyed some nights out

Bill Clinton, Václav Havel, Václav Klaus
REDUTA jazz club   11. 1. 1994

together and Clinton played his saxophone. (Look closely and you'll also see Madeleine Albright, a Czech emigré who served as Clinton's Secretary of State.) Upstairs at the same entrance is **Café Louvre**, a Parisian-style café and billiard hall where Franz

Kafka and Albert Einstein, among others, enjoyed a cup of coffee. It's a bright, cheery place to stop for a light lunch or some liquid refreshment.

The buzzing Café Louvre.

6 A few steps further down Národní, at the corner of **Spálená**, stands the country's most improbable cultural landmark: a **Tesco store**. Originally built during the 1970s as *Máj*, a communist-era department store, the building was remarkable for its Western style of architecture, rarely seen in Czechoslovakia at the time. After the Velvet Revolution it was briefly a K-Mart, and now serves as a refuge for countless expatriots who comb the shelves of the basement supermarket for imported food items unavailable anywhere else in the city. The Czech Cultural Ministry officially declared the building a landmark in the fall of 2006, upsetting Tesco managers who had been planning a major renovation. Now the building has to remain in its original condition.

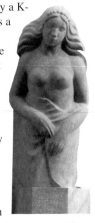

Watch out for charming details such as this shop-front's pillar.